Sound Doctrine

Volume II

C. R. Nichol
R. L. Whiteside

Gospel Advocate Company
P.O. Box 150
Nashville, Tennessee 37202

Original Title Page Text:

Sound Doctrine

A
SERIES OF BIBLE STUDES
FOR
SUNDAY SCHOOL CLASSES, PRAYER MEETINGS,
PRIVATE STUDY, COLLEGE CLASSES, Etc.

By
C. R. NICHOL and R. L. WHITESIDE

Vol. II

Sound Doctrine, Volume II
Gospel Advocate Reprints, 2001

© 1921, C. R. Nichol

Published by Gospel Advocate Co.
P.O. Box 150, Nashville, TN 37202
www.gospeladvocate.com
ISBN: 0-89225-481-5

SUBJECTS

	PAGE
Isaac, Jacob, Esau	7-17
Joseph	19-30
Deliverance of Israel From Bondage	31-42
Deliverance From Sin	43-53
The Ten Commandments	54-67
Prayer	68-81
The First Chapter of Acts	82-94
The Jerusalem Church	95-106
Conversion Of The Samaritans	107-119
Faith	120-131
Justification By Faith	132-141
Repentance	142-155
Partakers Of The Divine Nature	156-157

CONTENTS

                                                                            PAGE

A

Acceptable Prayer	74-77
Acts, Chapter 1	82-83
Alien Sinner's Prayer	77-78
Ananias and Sapphira	100
Ascension of Christ—to Pentecost	86-87

B

Baptized unto Moses. Baptized into Christ. Saved	47-48
Believe With All The Heart	125
Bible Teaching On Prayer	71

C

"Christian Graces."	159-164
Congregational Prayers	78
Conversion of the Samaritans	107

D

Deacons—the First	101-102
Deliverance Conditional	46
Deliverance From Sin	41
Deliverance of Israel From Bondage	31
Deliverers: Moses, Christ	44
Discipline	103
Dreams	11, 28

F

Faith	120-123
Faith, Degrees of	124
Faith, How it Comes	123-124
Faith, Justified by—Examples	138-139
Faith Only Does Not Save	126-129
False Ideas of the Kingdom	84, 85
Famine in Egypt and Palestine	23-27

CONTENTS

First Deacons 101, 102

H
Hebrew, Israelite, Jew 31
Historical Review 7

I
Isaac, Jacob, Esau 7
Isaac—Some Facts in His Life 9
Israelites Guided in Wilderness 48, 49
Israelite, Hebrew, Jew 31

J
Jacob Obtains Blessing 10
Jacob, Dream of 11
Jacob and Esau Reconciled 13
Jacob and Laban 12, 13
Jacob Loved, Esau Hated 15, 16
Jacob Sent From Home 11
Jacob Serves For Wives 11
Jerusalem and Christ's Ascension 85, 86
Jerusalem Church—Its Activities 96, 99
Jew 31
Joseph's Brethren go to Egypt 23-27
Joseph, His Dream 18, 19
Joseph Exalted 22
Joseph Sold 20, 21
Judas Iscariot 87-91

K
Kingdom, False Ideas About 84, 85

M
Moses 32-35
Moses and Aaron Before Pharoah 35
Many Fell 51
Mt. Sinai, Moral and Positive Law 54

O
Order of Faith and Repentance 150-153

P

Partakers of Divine Nature	156
Passover	36
Peter's Speech on Pentecost	89
Peter and John To Samaria	114-116
Pharoah's Dream	21
Philip Preaching Christ	108-111
Plagues in Egypt	36
Prayer, When Acceptable	74-77
Pray Always	74
Prayer, Bible Teaching On	71
Praying For Others	72, 73
Prayer of Alien Sinner	77, 78
Prayer, Some Hurtful Theories About	69-71

R

Repentance	143-149
Restitution	149, 150
Results of Philip's Preaching	111-113

S

Saved—Not By Faith Only	126-129
Simon	113-116
Some Facts in The Life of Isaac	9
Some Hurtful Theories About Prayer	69-71
Sowing and Reaping	14

T

Ten Commandments—To Whom Given	54, 55
Ten Commandments The Old Covenant	60-65
Tribes of Israel	31
Two Laws of Pardon	117

W

Waters Divide, Israel Saved	39

ISAAC, JACOB, AND ESAU.

METHODS OF STUDY. Two methods of study should be followed by every student of the Bible: (1) He should read and study the Bible closely from beginning to end. The purpose and contents of each book should be carefully noted. Some good maps and histories of the times will be valuable. (2) He should study by subjects. This is necessary if he would be successful in presenting the teaching of the Bible on any topic and be able to defend himself along any line. But if he studies altogether by subjects some of the most precious truths of the Bible will escape his attention, and he is likely to become lopsided, for he is sure to study some subjects to the neglect of others. Nothing takes the place of a thorough knowledge of the Bible as a whole. It is the purpose of the authors of "Sound Doctrine" to aid the student along both lines.

HISTORIC REVIEW. There are certain outstanding facts that we must keep well in mind. Frequent review is very helpful. In Vol. I. we had four historic lessons from the book of Genesis. (If you have not studied Vol. 1., you should secure a copy.) There are certain prominent facts in these lessons some of which help us to understand the New Testament. In the first chapter of Genesis we are told about the creation. Let us again note also: (1) God's first command to man (Gen. 1:28). (2) The creation of woman (Gen. 2:21, 22). The family instituted (Gen. 2:23, 24).

In the third chapter of Genesis is the account of the sin of Adam and Eve and their expulsion from the garden of Eden. Let us note: (1) The different ways the forbidden fruit appealed to Eve. (2) That Eve was deceived, Adam was not (I Tim. 2:14). That after sinning they might have lived on had they not been driven from the garden and away from the tree of life.

In the fourth chapter of Genesis we learn of Cain and Abel. "By faith Abel offered unto God a more excellent sacrifice than Cain, through which he had witness borne to him that he was righteous, God bearing witness in respect of his gifts: and through it he being dead yet speaketh" (Heb. 11:4).

In the sixth chapter of Genesis we have a record of the cause of the flood: "And Jehovah saw that the wickedness of man was great in the earth, and that every imagination of the thoughts of his heart was only evil continually..... And Jehovah said, I will destroy man whom I have created from the face of the ground" (vs. 5, 7).

After Noah the next outstanding figure in the development of God's plan is Abraham. The student should keep well in mind the promises made to Abraham when God called him out of Ur of the Chaldees (Gen. 12:1-3) and renewed at the offering of Isaac (Gen. 15-18), for all the rest of God's dealing with man as recorded in both the Old and New Testaments is but an unfolding and development of these promises. The covenant of circumcision is recorded in the seventeenth chapter of Genesis.

The student will observe that in the first eleven chapters of Genesis the writer gives a general history of the human family down to Abraham.

In Gen. 5:1-32 and 11:10-26 a regular line of patriarchs is given.

From the beginning of the twelfth chapter of Genesis to the close of the book the author deals mainly with individuals, and only with such individuals as have some relation to the development of the Hebrew nation.

ISAAC, JACOB, AND ESAU

SOME FACTS IN THE LIFE OF ISAAC.

1. Isaac was a child of promise (Gen. 17:15-19; Gal. 4:28).

2. Isaac was born when his father was one hundred years of age (Gen. 17:17; 21:1-5).

3. He was circumcised the eighth day (Gen. 21:4).

4. He was offered as a sacrifice (Gen. 22:1-8).

5. His mother died when he was thirty-seven years old (Gen. 17:17; 22:1-5).

6. Abraham sent his servant for a wife for Isaac (Gen. 24).

7. Isaac was forty years old when he married (Gen. 25:20).

8. His wife was barren, and he prayed for children (Gen. 25:21).

9. Esau and Jacob were born to him when he was sixty years old (Gen. 25:22-26).

10. The promises of God to Abraham (Gen. 12:1-3) were renewed to Isaac (Gen. 26:1-5). He was, therefore, in the line of patriarchs through whom Christ came.

11. He was a prosperous man (Gen. 26:12-16).

12. He was a man of peace, giving up his own rights for the sake of peace (Gen. 26:16-22).

13. He died at the age of one hundred and eighty years (Gen. 35:28, 29).

COMMENTS. The true greatness of these old-time heroes will be better appreciated if we remember that they had no books, none of the modern conveniences of civilization, and only meager revelations from Jehovah, and were surrounded by heathen darkness. But let us not forget that they were human and had their weaknesses. Through fear Isaac, as did Abraham, denied his wife, claiming that she was his siser (Gen. 26:6-11). Through all the trials, successes, and failures of Isaac he did not forget Jehovah (Gen. 26:23-25).

JACOB AND ESAU.

Jacob and Esau were twin sons of Isaac and Rebekah, but Esau was born first (Gen. 25:21-26). Isaac loved Esau, but Rebekah loved Jacob.

CHARACTER OF ESAU. Esau seems to have been a pleasure-loving sort of man, much given to fleshly indulgences and to acting on the impulse of the moment. Hence, when hungry, he sold his birthright to Jacob for a mess of pottage (Gen. 25:28-34). He was called a profane person (Heb. 12:16).

CHARACTER OF JACOB. Jacob, stern and inflexible, was determined in his purpose, so much so that he frequently yielded to the temptation to resort to tricks to obtain what he wanted. This kind of character, though not so pleasant and agreeable, is, under proper training and discipline, capable of a higher polish and of greater usefulness than that of the easy-going, pleasure-seeking Esau.

JACOB OBTAINS THE BLESSING. At Rebekah's suggestion and by her help, Jacob, by deception, obtained from Isaac the blessing meant for Esau (Gen. 27). When Esau learned this, "he cried with an exceeding great and bitter cry, and said unto his father, Bless me, even me also, O my father." He could not prevail on Isaac to change the blessing to him. Reference is made to this in Heb. 12:17. This verse as it appears in the King James Version has been the subject of much dispute, but the American Standard Version clears up the difficulty: "For ye know that even when he afterwards desired to inherit the blessing, he was rejected; for he found no place for a change of mind in his father, though he sought it diligently with tears."

ESAU'S ANGER. Esau became very angry, and vowed to kill Jacob after his father's death (Gen. 27:41). Rebekah advised Jacob to flee to her brother Laban, and tarry with him a few days, "until thy brother's

ISAAC, JACOB, AND ESAU

anger turn away from thee, and he forget that which thou hast done to him" (Gen. 27:43-45). Rebekah knew Esau's impulsive nature and that he would likely soon get over his anger.

JACOB SENT AWAY. Esau had married two Hittite women, "and they were a grief of mind unto Isaac and to Rebekah" (Gen. 26:34, 35). To gain Isaac's consent for Jacob to go away, she said to him: "I am weary of my life because of the daughters of Heth: if Jacob take a wife of the daughters of Heth, such as these, of the daughters of the land, what good shall my life do me? And Isaac called Jacob, and blessed him, and charged him, and said unto him, Thou shalt not take a wife of the daughters of Canaan. Arise and go to Paddan-aram, to the house of Bethuel thy mother's father, and take thee a wife from thence of the daughters of Laban thy mother's brother. And God Almighty bless thee, and make thee fruitful, and multiply thee, that thou mayest be a company of peoples; and give thee the blessing of Abraham, to thee, and to thy seed with thee; that thou mayest inherit the land of thy sojournings, which God gave unto Abraham" (Gen. 27:46; 28:1-4).

JACOB'S DREAM. While on his way to Paddan-aram Jacob had a wonderful dream, in which Jehovah appeared to him and renewed to him the promise made to Abraham and Isaac. This made a profound impression on Jacob, and he called the place Bethel ("House of God"), and vowed that if Jehovah would be with him and bless him, he would give the Lord a tenth of all that came into his hands (Gen. 28:6-22).

JACOB SERVES FOR LEAH AND RACHEL. When Jacob reached "the land of the children of the east," he found shepherds watering their flocks from a well. "And Jacob said unto them, My brethren, whence are ye? And they said, Of Haran are we. And he said unto them, Know ye Laban the son of Nahor? And they said, We know him. And he said unto them, Is it well with him? And they said, It is well; and, behold, Rachel his daughter cometh with the sheep..... While he was yet speaking with them, Rachel came with her father's sheep; for she kept them. And it came to pass, when Jacob saw Rachel the daughter of Laban his mother's brother, and the sheep of Laban his mother's brother, that Jacob went near, and rolled the stone from the well's mouth, and watered the flock of Laban his mother's brother. And Jacob kissed Rachel, and lifted up his voice, and wept. And Jacob told Rachel that he was her father's brother, and that he was Rebekah's son; and she ran and told her father" (Gen. 29:4-12).

"And Laban said unto Jacob, Because thou art my brother, shouldest thou therefore serve me for naught? tell me, what shall thy wages be? And Laban had two daughters: the name of the elder was Leah, and the name of the younger was Rachel. And Leah's eyes were tender; but Rachel was beautiful and well-favored. And Jacob loved Rachel, and he said, I will serve thee seven years for Rachel thy younger daughter. And Laban said, It is better that I give her to thee, than that I should give her to another man: abide with me. And Jacob served seven years for Rachel; and they seemed unto him but a few days, for the love he had to her" (Gen. 29:15-20). But Laban deceived Jacob and gave him Leah. Then Jacob served another seven years for Rachel (Gen. 29:21-30).

JACOB'S CHILDREN. In this land eleven sons—Reuben, Simeon, Levi, Judah, Dan, Naphtali, Gad, Asher, Issachar, Zebulun, and Joseph—and one daughter were born to Jacob (Gen. 29:31-35; 30:1-24).

JACOB BRINGS PROSPERITY TO LABAN. "And it came to pass, when Rachel had borne Joseph, that Jacob said unto Laban, Send me away, that I may go unto mine own place, and to my country. Give me my wives and my children for whom I have served thee, and let me go: for thou knowest my service wherewith I have served thee. And Laban said unto him, If now I have found favor in thine eyes, tarry: for I have divined that Jehovah hath blessed me for thy sake. And he said, Appoint me thy wages, and I will give it. And he said unto him, Thou knowest how I have served thee, and how thy cattle have fared with me. For it was little which thou hadst before I came, and it hath increased unto a multitude; and Jehovah hath blessed thee whithersoever I turned: and now when shall I provide for mine own house also?" (Gen. 30:25-30).

JACOB WORKS FOR A SHARE OF THE CATTLE. Laban and Jacob entered into a contract which provided that for his services to Laban Jacob was to receive all the off colors amongst the flocks and herds. This gave Jacob an opportunity to practice some more of his trickery, by which he became very prosperous. "And the man increased exceedingly, and had large flocks, and maidservants and men-servants, and camels and asses" (Gen. 30:43).

JACOB'S DEPARTURE. "And he heard the words of Laban's sons, saying, Jacob hath taken away all that was our father's; and of that which was our father's hath he gotten all this glory. And Jacob beheld the countenance of Laban, and, behold, it was not toward him as beforetime. And Jehovah said unto Jacob, Return unto the land of thy fathers, and to thy kindred; and I will be with thee" (Gen. 31:1-3). Jacob then took his family and his possessions, and departed "to go to Isaac his father unto the land of Canaan."

JACOB AND ESAU RECONCILED. While enroute Jacob sent messengers to Esau seeking his favor. Their report that Esau was coming to meet him with four hundred armed men aroused in Jacob great fear and distress, and he prayed earnestly to Jehovah for protection (Gen.

32:1-12). Knowing Esau's nature, Jacob sent rich gifts on before to Esau, that he might turn his anger away (Gen. 32:13-21). That night he remained behind, and wrestled with an angel, who gave him the name "Israel." When he met Esau next day, a complete reconciliation resulted (Gen. 33:1-15). Esau returned to Seir, and Jacob went on to Succoth, then to Shechem (Gen. 33:16-20).

JACOB BUILDS ALTAR AT BETHEL. "And God said unto Jacob, Arize, go up to Bethel, and dwell there: and make there an altar unto God, who appeared unto thee when thou fleddest from the face of Esau thy brother." Having put away their idols, Jacob and his family went up to Bethel, where he builded an altar (Gen. 35:1-8). On their way from Bethel to Ephrath, Benjamin was born and Rachel died (Gen. 35:16-20). After the death of Isaac, Esau graciously left the rich grazing lands to Jacob and withdrew to Mount Seir, where his descendants developed into a kingdom.

JACOB'S LAST DAYS. The last days of Jacob's life are so closely connected with Joseph that it is easier to present the leading incidents of that part of his life in the lesson of Joseph. This will be found in the next lesson.

SOME REFLECTIONS AND COMMENTS.

SOWING AND REAPING. "Whatsoever a man soweth, that shall he also reap" (Gal. 6:7). This universal law of nature Paul applies to the spiritual and moral life. Jacob's history is a striking illustration of this law. He deceived his father in the blindness of his old age, and was deceived by Laban, who gave him Leah instead of Rachel whom he loved and for whom he labored seven years. Later, by deception, his own sons led him to believe Joseph had been destroyed by a wild beast. Was not Jacob reaping as he had sown? We do not intend to convey the idea that a man receives the judgment for his sins in this life, but is it not true that man often reaps in this life from seeds of his own sowing? Can you recall such experiences in your own life or the lives of others?

LOVED JACOB, HATED ESAU. "Rebekah also having conceived by one, even by our father Isaac—for the children being not yet born, neither having done anything good or bad, that the purpose of God according to election might stand, not of works, but of him that calleth, it was said unto her, The elder shall serve the younger. Even as it is written, Jacob have I loved, but Esau I hated" (Rom. 9:10-13). This election had nothing to do with the salvation of either Jacob or Esau, but was only God's choice that upon Jacob should descend the promise made to Abraham (Gen. 12:1-3), and renewed to Isaac (Gen. 26:2-5). It put Jacob in the line of the patriarchs through whom the promise should be fulfilled.

THE ELDER SHALL SERVE THE YOUNGER. Before they were born it was said: "The elder shall serve the younger." But this could not have been spoken of Jacob and Esau as individuals, for the reverse came nearer being true of them as individuals. Jacob, the younger, feared Esau, calling him lord, and referred to himself as Esau's servant (Gen. 33:1-15). The statement, "The elder shall serve the younger," is quoted from Jehovah's speech to Rebekah: "Two nations are in thy womb, and two peoples shall be separated from thy bowels: and the one people shall be stronger than the other people; and the elder shall serve the younger" (Gen. 25:23). "Two nations"—"two peoples." The language shows clearly that the elder people, or nation, were to serve the younger people, or nation; and it is a fact that the elder people, or nation, did serve the younger, as Jehovah had said (II Sam. 8:14).

JACOB I LOVED, BUT ESAU I HATED. In the passage under consideration Paul quotes from widely different passages of scripture. "The elder shall serve the younger" was spoken by Jehovah to Rebekah before the children were born (Gen. 25:23); but, long years after Jacob and Esau were dead, God said: "Jacob I loved, but Esau I hated" (Mal. 1:1-3). Even here the verses which follow show that God spoke of the two nations, rather than of Jacob and Esau as individuals, for he said: "Whereas Edom saith, We are beaten down, but we will return and build the waste places; thus saith Jehovah of hosts, they shall build, but I will throw down; and men shall call them The border of wickedness, and The people against whom Jehovah hath indignation forever" (Mal. 1:4). "We"—"they"—"them" —"the people." Such language shows that God was speaking of two nations instead of Jacob and Esau as individuals.

* * *

TOPICS FOR INVESTIGATION AND DISCUSSION.

The Life of Abraham.
Sacrificing Personal Right for Peace.
The Character of Esau.
The Character of Jacob.
Election and Reprobation.

* * *

QUESTIONS.

1. What two methods of Bible study can you recommend?
2. Give benefits of each.
3. Give the work of the days of creation in order.
4. What was God's first command to man?
5. What was man's work in the garden?
6. What was his food?
7. Tell why the forbidden fruit appealed to them?
8. Why were they driven from the garden?
9. What offerings did Cain and Abel bring?

ISAAC, JACOB, AND ESAU

10. Why was Abel's accepted and Cain's rejected?
11. Why did God send the flood?
12. Tell how Noah was saved by God, faith, ark, water.
13. Where did God appear to Abraham?
14. Repeat the promises found in Gen. 12:1-3.
15. What is meant by "seed" in Gen. 12:1-3? Give New Testament proof.
16. How old was Abraham when this promise was made?
17. Into what land did Abraham go?
18. In the covenant of circumcision, what did God promise Abraham?
19. How old was Abraham when the covenant of circumcision was made?
20. How old was Abraham at his death?
21. Name the leading trait in Abraham's character.
22. How old was Abraham at Isaac's birth?
23. How old was Isaac when circumcised?
24. Give an account of Isaac being offered as a sacrifice.
25. Tell how Abraham procured a wife for Isaac.
26. What do you think of the faith and confidence of the servant who was sent to find a wife for Isaac?
27. Who was Isaac's wife?
28. What kin were Isaac and his wife?
29. How old was Isaac when he married?
30. For what did Isaac pray?
31. What names were given the children?
32. What was Isaac's age at the birth of the children?
33. What promises made to Abraham were renewed to Isaac?
34. To what age did Isaac live?
35. What can you say of Isaac's character?
36. Why remarkable that some men of that age developed such remarkable characters?
37. Mention some indications of human weakness in Isaac.
38. Tell of Isaac's sacrifice for peace.
39. Why did Isaac love Esau?
40. What trade did Jacob make with Esau?
41. What does the word "profane" mean?
42. Why was Esau called a profane person?
43. Give difference in characters of Jacob and Esau.
44. Tell how Jacob and his mother deceived Isaac.
45. How did this affect Esau?
46. What threat did he make?
47. Whom had Esau married?

18 SOUND DOCTRINE

48. How did Rebekah gain Isaac's consent for Jacob to go away?
49. Tell Jacob's dream on the way.
50. What name did he give the place, and why?
51. What vow did he make?
52. Tell of the conversation and incidents at the well.
53. To whose house did he go?
54. What is said of the two daughters?
55. With whom did Jacob fall in love?
56. On what condition might he have her for a wife?
57. How was he deceived, and what excuse was given?
58. How long did he then serve for Rachel?
59. What the number and names of the children born to him in that land?
60. After Joseph's birth, what conversation between Laban and Jacob?
61. To what did Leban attribute his prosperity?
62. What liberal proposition did Laban make Jacob?
63. What did Jacob propose to accept as wages?
64. What is said of Jacob's possessions?
65. Is it sinful to be wealthy?
66. Can you name any other Bible characters who were wealthy?
67. How did Laban and his sons regard Jacob now?
68. What did Jehovah command Jacob to do?
69. Tell of his departure to Canaan.
70. How did Esau prepare to meet Jacob?
71. What were Jacob's feelings, and what did he do?
72. What other name was given him, and why?
73. What resulted from the meeting of Jacob and Esau?
74. To what place did Esau return?
75. Where did Jacob build an altar?
76. Where was Benjamin born?
77. Into what kingdom did Esau and his descendants develop?
78. Show how Jacob reaped as he had sown.
79. What the meaning of "Jacob have I loved?"
80. What the meaning of "The elder shall serve the younger?"

JOSEPH.

Eleven sons, of whom Joseph was the youngest, were born to Jacob in Paddan-aram, whither Jacob had fled from the wrath of his brother Esau. Joseph was the first son of Jacob's most loved wife, Rachel. Benjamin, the other son of Rachel, and the youngest son of Jacob was born during their journey back to Jacob's father, Isaac (Gen. 36:16-20).

JACOB'S FAVORITE SON. Joseph was the favorite son of Jacob. "Now Israel loved Joseph more than all his children, because he was the son of his old age: and he made him a coat of many colors" (Gen. 37:3). Favoritism in a family, even though there be natural and just grounds for it, is almost sure to bring anything but happy results. It brought disturbance into Jacob's family and years of sorrow to him in his old age. It embittered Joseph's brethren, and perhaps stirred in him a feeling of superiority. "And his brethren saw that their father loved him more than all his brethren; and they hated him, and could not speak peaceably unto him" (Gen. 37:4).

JOSEPH'S DREAMS. He dreamed a dream, and told it to his brethren. "We were binding sheaves in the field, and, lo, my sheaf arose, and also stood upright; and, behold, your sheaves came round about, and made obeisance to my sheaf. And his brethren said to him, Shalt thou indeed reign over us? or shalt thou indeed have dominion over us? And they hated him yet the more for his dreams, and for his words" (Gen. 37:5-8). He related another dream: "Behold, I have dreamed yet a dream; and, behold, the sun and the moon and eleven stars made obeisance to me. And he told it to his father, and to his brethren; and his father rebuked him, and said unto him, What is this dream that thou hast dreamed? Shall I and thy mother and thy brethren indeed come to bow down ourselves to thee to the earth? And his brethren envied him; but his father kept the saying in mind" (Gen. 37:9-11).

VISITS HIS BRETHREN. His brethren went to Shechem to tend their father's flocks. To learn how they fared, Jacob said to Joseph: "Go now, see whether it is well with the brethren, and well with the flock; and bring me word again." Arriving at Shechem, Joseph found that his brethren had gone to Dothan, and he departed thence to find them (see Gen. 37:12-17).

THE CONSPIRACY. When he came in sight of his brethren, they said, "Behold, this dreamer cometh," and they conspired to slay him. But Reuben, the oldest brother, persuaded them to cast him into a pit, intending to rescue him and send him back home. Having stripped Joseph of his coat of many colors, they cast him into an empty pit (see Gen. 37:18-24).

JOSEPH SOLD. In the absence of Reuben the others sold Joseph to a caravan of merchantmen, who took him down into Egypt and sold him to Potiphar, captain of Pharaoh's guard. They dipped Joseph's coat in the blood of a kid and carried it to Jacob, who accepted it as evidence that Joseph had been killed by a wild beast (see Gen. 37:25-36). Jacob was deceived, but his sorrow was genuine.

IN POTIPHAR'S HOUSE. Joseph was so faithful, and things prospered so in his hands, that Potiphar soon made him overseer in his house. "And it came to pass from the time that he made him overseer in his house, and over all that he had, that Jehovah blessed the Egyptian's house for Joseph's sake; and the blessing of Jehovah was upon all that he had, in the house and in the field. And he left all that he had in Joseph's hand;

and he knew not aught that was with him, save the bread which he did eat" (Gen. 39:5, 6).

IMPRISONED. "Joseph was comely, and well-favored." Potiphar's wife became enamored with him. Failing in her sinful scheme, she falsely accused Joseph, and he was cast into prison, "the place where the king's prisoners were bound" (see Gen. 39:7-26).

A FAVORITE IN PRISON. "But Jehovah was with Joseph, and showed kindness unto him, and gave him favor in the sight of the keeper of the prison. And the keeper of the prison committed to Joseph's hand all the prisoners that were in the prison; and whatsoever they did there, he was the doer of it" (Gen. 39:21, 22).

PHARAOH'S CHIEF BUTLER AND BAKER. Pharaoh's chief butler and chief baker were cast into prison, "the place where Joseph was bound." "And the captain of the guard charged Joseph with them." Both dreamed dreams which troubled them greatly, for there was no one to interpret them. "And Joseph said unto them, Do not interpretations belong to God? tell it me, I pray you." The chief butler related his dream, "and Joseph said unto him ..... within yet three days shall Pharaoh lift up thy head, and restore thee thine office." Then Joseph begged the butler to make an effort with Pharaoh in his behalf. The chief baker related his dream, which Joseph interpreted to mean that within three days the baker would be hanged. "Yet did not the chief butler remember Joseph, but forgat him" (see Gen. 40).

PHARAOH'S DREAMS. Pharaoh dreamed that seven fat cattle came up out of the river and were eaten up by seven lean-fleshed cattle which came up after them. He dreamed again that seven good ears of grain which grew on one stalk were swallowed up by seven thin and blasted ears which grew up after them. Pharaoh was troubled; and none of the magicians and wise men of Egypt, when called, could interpret his dreams. Then the chief butler remembered his ingratitude toward Joseph and told of the dreams in prison, of their interpretation by Joseph, and of their fulfillment according to Joseph's interpretation (see Gen. 41:1-13).

JOSEPH RELEASED — INTERPRETS PHARAOH'S DREAMS. Joseph was brought hastily out of the dungeon, and appeared before Pharaoh, who then related his dreams to Joseph. "And Joseph said unto Pharaoh, The dream of Pharaoh is one: what God is about to do he hath declared unto Pharaoh. The seven good kine are seven years; and the seven good ears are seven years: the dream is one. And the seven lean and ill-favored kine that came up after them are seven years, and also the seven empty ears blasted with the east wind; they shall be seven years of famine. That is the thing which I spake unto Pharaoh: what God is about to do he hath showed unto Pharaoh. Behold, there come seven years of great plenty throughout all the land of Egypt: and there shall arise after them seven years of famine; and all the plenty shall be forgotten in the land of Egypt; and the famine shall consume the land; and the plenty shall not be known in the land by reason of that famine which followeth; for it shall be very grievous. And for that the dream was doubled unto Pharaoh, it is because the thing is established by God, and God will shortly bring it to pass" (see Gen. 41:14-32).

JOSEPH EXALTED. Joseph advised Pharaoh to set a capable man over all Egypt, that a fifth part of the products of the land might be laid up during the seven plenteous years for food during the seven years of famine. Pharaoh, having decided that none other was so wise and discreet as Joseph, appointed him ruler over all the land; only Pharaoh was to be greater than he (Gen. 41:33-44).

JOSEPH'S WIFE AND SONS. Asenath, daughter of Potiphera, priest of On, became Joseph's wife. To them were born two sons, Manasseh and Ephraim (Gen. 41: 45, 51, 52).

THE FAMINE. The seven years of plenty were followed by seven years of famine in which nothing was made in Egypt. The famine extended into other countries (Gen. 41:53, 54).

JOSEPH'S BRETHREN COME TO BUY FOOD. The famine extended up into the land of Canaan, where Jacob dwelt. Having learned of the stores of grain in Egypt, Jacob sent his sons down to buy food. Benjamin remained with his father.

When the ten brothers came into Joseph's presence, he recognized them; but they did not know him, and he did not make himself known to them.

In studying this narrative let us remember that Joseph was human, and that he had suffered greatly at the hands of his brethren. He could not know but that his brethren had told his father the truth about his disappearance, and perhaps he felt that his father had not tried very hard to find him. It is no wonder, then, that he spoke roughly to them and accused them of being spies, and that he remembered his dreams. They protested their innocence. "And Joseph said unto them, That is it that I spake unto you, saying, Ye are spies: hereby ye shall be proved: by the life of Pharaoh ye shall not go forth hence, except your youngest brother come hither. Send one of you, and let him fetch your brother, and ye shall be bound, that your words may be proved, whether there be truth in you: or else by the life of Pharaoh surely ye are spies. And he put them all together into ward three days." It is plain that he was laying a plan to have Benjamin brought down and let the rest go. It will be remembered that Joseph and Benjamin were full brothers, the only sons of Rachel.

On the third day of their imprisonment Joseph proposed that one be bound as a pledge that they would bring their youngest brother down. "And they did so. And they said one to another, We are verily guilty concerning our brother, in that we saw the distress of his soul, when he besought us, and we would not hear: therefore is this distress come upon us. And Reuben answered them, saying, Spake I not unto you, saying, Do not sin against the child; and ye would not hear? therefore also, behold, his blood is required. And they knew not that Joseph understood them; for there was an interpreter between them." Reuben was the oldest, and would likely have been bound, but Joseph learned from his speech that he was not as quilty as were the others. Simeon, the next oldest, was bound before their eyes and kept as a guaranty that they would bring Benjamin. "Then Joseph commanded to fill their vessels with grain, and to restore every man's money into his sack, and to give them provision for the way: and thus was it done unto them" (Gen. 42:1-25).

THEIR RETURN HOME. When they reached home, they reported to their father Jacob their experiences and their rough treatment at the hands of the lord of the land and their promise to bring Benjamin. "And Jacob their father said unto them, Me have ye bereaved of my children: Joseph is not, and Simeon is not, and ye will take Benjamin away: all these things are against me. And Reuben spake unto his father, saying, Slay my two sons, if I bring him not unto thee: deliver him into my hand, and I will bring him to thee again. And he said, My son shall not go down with you; for his brother is dead, and he only is left: if harm befall him by the way in which ye go, then will ye bring down my gray hairs with sorrow to Sheol" (see Gen. 42:26-38).

THE SECOND JOURNEY. When their supplies were exhausted, Jacob said to them: "Go again, buy a little food." Judah replied: "If thou wilt send our brother with us, we will go down and buy thee food; but if

thou wilt not send him, we will not go down; for the
man said unto us, Ye shall not see my face, except your
brother be with you." Jacob said: "Wherefore dealt ye
so ill with me as to tell the man whether ye had yet a
brother?" Judah replied that the man asked them
plainly if they had another brother, and that they could
not know he would say: "Bring your brother down."
Judah promised to be surety for Benjamin, and Jacob
sent them away with presents for the man and the
money that had been returned in their sacks, saying:
"God Almighty give you mercy before the man, that he
may release unto you your brother and Benjamin."
"And when Joseph saw Benjamin with them, he said
to the steward of his house, Bring the men into the
house, and slay, and make ready; for the men shall dine
with me at noon." "And the men were afraid, because
they were brought to Joseph's house; and they said,
Because of the money that was returned in our sacks
at the first time are we brought in; that ye may seek
occasion against us, and fall upon us, and take us for
bondmen, and our asses." They went before the steward
of Joseph's house and plead their innocence, and that
they had brought again the money which they found in
their sacks. The steward replied: "Peace be to you,
fear not: your God, and the God of your father hath
given you treasure in your sacks: I had your money."
Simeon was brought out of the prison, and everything
was made ready for their meeting Joseph at the noon
meal, for they were to eat with him. When Joseph came
in, he asked: "Is your father well, the old man of whom
ye spake? Is he yet alive? And they said, Thy servant
our father is well, he is yet alive. And they bowed
the head, and made obeisance. And he lifted up his
eyes, and saw Benjamin his brother, his mother's son,
and said, Is this your youngest brother, of whom ye
spake unto me? And he said, God be gracious unto

thee, my son. And Joseph made haste; for his heart yearned over his brother: and he sought where to weep, and he entered into his chamber, and wept there. And he washed his face, and came out; and he refrained himself, and said, Set on bread." They were arranged at the table according to their ages, which caused them to marvel. Benjamin's portion was five times as much as any of the others (Gen. 43).

THEY START HOME. When they were ready to start home, Joseph commanded the steward to put every man's money into his sack, and to put his silver cup into Benjamin's sack. When they had gone but a little way, the steward, at the command of Joseph, followed them, and accused them of taking Joseph's cup. They protested their innocence, reminding him that they had brought back the money previously found in their sacks. How then should we steal out of thy lord's house silver or gold?" The steward said: "He with whom it is found shall be my bondman; and ye shall be blameless." The cup was found in Benjamin's sack. It seems plain that Joseph was planning to keep Benjamin and let the others return. They all hastily returned to Joseph's house, and "fell before him on the ground." And Joseph said unto them: "What deed is this that ye have done? know ye not that such a man as I can indeed divine? And Judah said, What shall we say unto my lord? what shall we speak? or how shall we clear ourselves? God hath found out the iniquity of thy servants: behold, we are my lord's bondmen, both we, and he also in whose hand the cup is found. And he said, Far be it from me that I should do so: the man in whose hand the cup is found, he shall be my bondman; but as for you, get you up in peace unto your father."

Then Judah made a very tender and touching appeal, in which he related that his father all these years had mourned Joseph as dead, and that his father was now so devoted to Benjamin that his loss would cause his father's death, and closed with these words: "For thy servant became surety for the lad unto my father, saying, If I bring him not unto thee, then shall I bear the blame to my father forever. Now therefore, let thy servant, I pray thee, abide instead of the lad a bondman to my lord; and let the lad go up with his brethren. For how shall I go up to my father, if the lad be not with me? lest I see the evil that shall come on my father." This speech revealed Joseph's brethren in a new light. They were no longer cruel and heartless, as they were when, despite his pleading and anguish of soul, they had sold him as a slave. Years had mellowed them; and now, although Benjamin was Jacob's favorite as Joseph had been, yet they, instead of being resentful, were very tender toward both Benjamin and their father. Joseph's sternness departed—he was completely overcome. He made himself known to his astonished and bewildered brethren. "And he said, I am Joseph your brother, whom ye sold into Egypt. And now be not grieved, nor angry with yourselves, that ye sold me hither: for God did send me before you to preserve life" (Gen. 44:1-34; 45:1-8).

SENDS FOR HIS FATHER JACOB. His brethren sent in haste for Jacob their father. Tidings having reached Pharaoh, he provided richly for their journey, and promised them the fat of the land when they returned with their father and their families. When they arrived home, Jacob could hardly believe the report till he saw the wagons which were brought to carry them back into Egypt (Gen. 45:9-28).

JACOB AND FAMILY ALL GO DOWN INTO EGYPT. In their journey into Egypt they camped at Beer-sheba, and Jacob "offered sacrifices unto the God of his father Isaac." Here God appeared to him, and promised to protect him during his sojourn in Egypt and to bring him again out of the land.

When they reached Egypt, Pharaoh assigned them the land of Goshen for a home, and they were cared for during the famine (Gen. 46, 47).

THE TRIBES OF ISRAEL. Before his death Jacob blessed each of his sons. Each son became the head of a tribe, excepting Joseph, whose two sons, Ephraim and Manasseh, each became the head of a tribe (Gen. 48, 49).

DREAMS. The part dreams have had as a means of communicating God's mind to men is a matter of interest to every Bible student. Such dreams fall into three divisions: (1) An angel speaks to man in a dream; (2) communication is made to the dreamer by what appears to be the distinct voice of Jehovah; (3) the dreamer sees in his dream a vision or visions.

The following dreams come under the first division: Matt. 1:20; 2:13; 2:19.

Dreams coming under the second division are mentioned in Gen. 20:3; 31:24; I Kings 3:4, 5.

In each of these classes there was little difficulty in understanding the revelation, for the message was spoken distinctly either by an angel or by the Lord himself.

In the third class the dreamer saw a vision which to his mind was a mystery. Some divinely qualified man must interpret these dreams. The following are some of the dreams of this class: The dreams of the chief butler and the chief baker (Gen. 40), the dreams of Pharaoh (Gen. 41:1-32), and the dream of Nebuchadnezzar (Dan. 2:1-45). The interpretations were of God. But this raises a question: If the interpretations were of God, were not the dreams also? But in what way, or by what means, did God so impress these men as to cause them to dream prophetic dreams? The answer to this question is one of the secret things that belong to God.

JOSEPH

TOPICS FOR INVESTIGATION AND DISCUSSION.

Evils of Favoritism in the Family.
Seeming Calamities Sometimes a Blessing.
Joseph as a Character Study.
Religion of the Egyptians in Joseph's Time.
Dreams.

* * *

QUESTIONS.

1. Name Jacob's sons.
2. Who was Joseph's mother?
3. Why did Jacob love Joseph most?
4. How did he manifest his love?
5. How did this affect the other sons?
6. What effect on Joseph?
7. Relate Joseph's dreams.
8. How did they affect his brethren?
9. What did Jacob say?
10. Where did Jacob send Joseph, and why?
11. Where did he find his brethren?
12. What did his brethren say when they saw him?
13. What did they first plan to do?
14. Who objected, and what did he suggest?
15. What purpose did he have in suggesting this?
16. How did the others finally dispose of Joseph?
17. Who were the Ishmaelites?
18. How did they deceive Jacob?
19. To whom did the Ishmaelites sell Joseph?
20. How did Joseph's master regard him?
21. What caused his imprisonment?
22. How did he stand as a prisoner?
23. What prominent men were put into prison?
24. Relate the butler's dream and Joseph's interpretation.
25. Relate the baker's dream and Joseph's interpretation.
26. What did Joseph request the butler to do?
27. Tell Pharaoh's dreams.
28. Of whom did he first seek an interpretation?
29. Tell how Joseph's imprisonment was a means of bringing him before Pharaoh.
30. What interpretation did he give to Pharaoh's dreams?
31. What advice did he give Pharaoh?

32. Why did Pharaoh select Joseph for the place?
33. To whom was Joseph married?
34. Name his sons.
35. What part of the grain was collected during the years of plenty?
36. How extensive was the famine?
37. Discuss the significance of this: They lived seven years on one-fifth of what they had during the years of plenty.
38. Why did Joseph's brethren come down?
39. How did Joseph treat them?
40. How do you account for his conduct toward them?
41. How long did he keep them bound?
42. What did Joseph finally propose to do?
43. Who was bound and kept, and why?
44. Why not Reuben, as he was the oldest?
45. What did they find in their sacks of grain?
46. When they reported to Jacob their promise to bring Benjamin, what did he say?
47. When their supplies were exhausted what did Jacob say?
48. Outline the conversation that followed.
49. When Jacob relented, what instructions did he give?
50. Tell how they were received at the house of Joseph.
51. When Joseph came in, what inquiries did he make?
52. How was Joseph affected at the sight of Benjamin?
53. What plan did Joseph fall on to keep Benjamin?
54. When they all returned, what did Joseph propose?
55. Outline Judah's speech—give his closing appeal.
56. What effect did it have on Joseph?
57. What change in his brethren did he now discover?
58. Tell how he made himself known to his brethren.
59. Whom did he say had sent him into Egypt, and why?
60. What did he tell his brethren to do?
61. What effect did their report have on Jacob?
62. What caused him to believe?
63. Where did they locate in Egypt?
64. What are the tribes of Israel?
65. What charge did Jacob give concerning his burial?
66. How long did Joseph live?
67. Name three classes of dreams found in the Bible.
68. Which class had to be interpreted?
69. Did God through these dreams reveal any new law to any one?

DELIVERANCE OF HEBREWS FROM BONDAGE

LESSON TEXT: Exodus, first fifteen chapters.

MEMORY VERSES: Heb. 11:29.

HEBREW—ISRAELITE—JEW.

HEBREW. The name "Hebrew" was first applied to Abraham (Gen. 14:13). Later it was applied to that part of his descendants who went down into Egypt (Gen. 39:14; Ex. 1:19; 2:6, 7). After this the name was often applied to God's chosen people.

ISRAEL, ISRAELITE. The name "Israel" was first given to Jacob by the angel who wrestled with him by the brook Jabbok (Gen. 32:22-28). Jacob was the grandson of Abraham, and his family was that part of Abraham's descendants who went down into Egypt and were called Hebrews. The descendants of Jacob were frequently also called the children of Israel, Israelites, or simply Israel.

JEWS. After the kingdom was divided under the reign of Rehoboam (I Kings 12:1-16), the tribes of Judah and Benjamin remained with Rehoboam, and his government was known as the kingdom of Judah. Those who went with Jeroboam were called the kingdom of Israel. During this divided condition the people of the kingdom of Judah were sometimes called Jews. Since the return of the Hebrews from the Babylonian captivity the name "Jew" has been applied to all the Israelites, regardless of their tribal relations (Esther 2:5).

THE TRIBES OF ISRAEL.

The descendants of each of the sons of Jacob constituted a tribe, excepting Joseph, whose two sons, Ephraim and Manasseh, each became the head of a tribe.

THE HARDSHIPS AND GROWTH OF THE HEBREWS.

The Hebrews were very few when they went down into Egypt, but they multiplied so rapidly that they soon became a great multitude (Ex. 1:1-7). For some time they were treated well; but after the death of Joseph the government changed hands, and there followed a series of oppressions against the Hebrews to keep them from multiplying so rapidly. They had taskmasters over them, who made them serve with rigor, and their lives became bitter; but the more they were oppressed, the more they grew (Ex. 1:8-13). The midwives were commanded to kill all the sons born to the Hebrews (Ex. 1:15-22).

MOSES.

While the decree was in force to slay all the male children born to the Hebrews, Moses was born to Amram and Jochebed of the tribe of Levi (Ex. 2:1-10; 6:20). To save Moses, his parents hid him three months (Ex. 2:2; Acts 7:20, 21). "By faith Moses, when he was born, was hid three months by his parents, because they saw he was a goodly child; and they were not afraid of the king's commandment" (Heb. 11:23). How he finally fell into the hands of the king's daughter and was brought up as her son is told in Ex. 2:3-10.

HIS EARLY TRAINING. In Pharaoh's house Moses "was instructed in all wisdom of the Egyptians, and was mighty in word and work" (Acts 7:22). But he did not forget his people—the impressions made on him by his mother in the few brief years that he was with her were never erased. "By faith Moses, when he was grown up, refused to be called the son of Pharaoh's daughter;

choosing rather to share ill treatment with the people of God, than to enjoy the pleasures of sin for a season; accounting the reproach of Christ greater riches than the treasures of Egypt: for he looked unto the recompense of reward" (Heb. 11:24-26).

His Flight to Midian. "When he was well-nigh forty years old, it came into his heart to visit his brethren the children of Israel. And seeing one of them suffer wrong, he defended him, and avenged him that was oppressed, smiting the Egyptian: and he supposed that his brethren understood that God by his hand was giving them deliverance; but they understood not. And the day following he appeared unto them as they strove, and would have set them at one again, saying, Sirs, ye are brethren; why do ye wrong one to another? But he that did his neighbor wrong thrust him away, saying, Who made thee a ruler and a judge over us? Wouldest thou kill me as thou killedst the Egyptian yesterday? And Moses fled at this saying, and became a sojourner in the land of Midian, where he begat two sons. And when forty years were fulfilled, an angel appeared to him in the wilderness of Mount Sinai, in a flame of fire in a bush. And when Moses saw it, he wondered at the sight: and as he drew near to behold, there came a voice of the Lord, I am the God of thy fathers, the God of Abraham, and of Isaac, and of Jacob. And Moses trembled, and durst not behold. And the Lord said unto him, Loose the shoes from thy feet: for. the place whereon thou standest is holy ground. I have surely seen the affliction of my people that is in Egypt, and have heard their groaning, and I am come down to deliver them: and now come, I will send thee into Egypt. This Moses whom they refused, saying, Who made thee a ruler and a judge? him hath God sent to be both a ruler and a deliverer with the hand of the angel that appeared to him in the bush. This man led them forth, having wrought wonders and signs in Egypt, and in the Red Sea, and in the wilderness forty years" (Acts 7:23:36).

GOD'S CALL TO MOSES. When God appeared to Moses in the land of Midian, he said: "I will send thee unto Pharaoh, that thou mayest bring forth my people the children of Israel out of Egypt." Feeling unequal to the task, Moses said: "Who am I that I should go unto Pharaoh, and that I should bring forth the children of Israel out of Egypt?" (Ex. 3:10, 11). But God replied: "Certainly I will be with thee." Again Moses objected, saying: "Behold, they will not believe me, nor hearken unto my voice; for they will say, Jehovah hath not appeared unto thee" (Ex. 4:1). Jehovah then gave Moses two signs to perform before the people to convince them that God was with them, adding: "If they will not believe even these two signs, neither hearken unto thy voice, then thou shalt take of water of the river, and pour it upon the dry land: and the water which thou takest out of the river shall become blood upon the dry land" (Ex. 4:2-9). Again Moses objected: "Oh, Lord, I am not eloquent, neither heretofore, nor since thou hast spoken unto thy servant; for I am slow of speech, and of a slow tongue. And Jehovah said unto him, Who hath made man's mouth? or who maketh a man dumb, or deaf, or seeing, or blind? is it not I Jehovah? Now therefore go, and I will be with thy mouth, and teach thee what thou shalt speak. And he said, Oh, Lord, send, I pray thee, by the hand of him whom thou wilt send. And the anger of Jehovah was kindled against Moses, and he said, Is there not Aaron thy brother the Levite? I know that he can speak well. And also, behold, he cometh forth to meet thee: and when he seeth thee, he will be glad in his heart. And thou shalt speak unto him, and put the words in his mouth: and I will be with thy mouth, and with his mouth, and will teach you what ye shall do. And he shall be thy spokesman unto the people; and it shall come to pass, that he shall be to thee a mouth, and thou shalt be to him as God. And thou shalt take in thy hand this rod, wherewith thou shalt do the signs" (Ex. 4:10-17).

"And Moses and Aaron went and gathered together all the elders of the children of Israel: and Aaron spake all the words which Jehovah had spoken unto Moses, and did the signs in the sight of the people. And the people believed: and when they heard that Jehovah had visited the children of Israel, and that he had seen their afflictions, then they bowed their heads and worshipped" (Ex. 4:29-31).

THEY GO TO PHARAOH. "And afterward Moses and Aaron came, and said unto Pharaoh, Thus saith Jehovah, the God of Israel, Let my people go, that they may hold a feast unto me in the wilderness. And Pharaoh said, Who is Jehovah, that I should hearken unto his voice to let Israel go? I know not Jehovah, and moreover I will not let Israel go" (Ex. 5:1, 2). Pharaoh accused Moses and Aaron of hindering the people from their work, and sent them away. He then commanded the taskmasters to make the burdens heavier for the people. The people blamed Moses and Aaron for the increased hardships (Ex. 5:20, 21).

The Lord sent Moses and Aaron back to Pharaoh with signs to perform before him. "And Moses and Aaron went in unto Pharaoh, and they did so, as Jehovah had commanded: and Aaron cast down his rod before Pharaoh and before his servants, and it became a serpent. Then Pharaoh also called for the wise men and the sorcerers: and they also, the magicians of Egypt, did in like manner with their enchantments. For they cast down every man his rod, and they became serpents; but Aaron's rod swallowed up their rods. And Pharaoh's heart was hardened, and he hearkened not unto them; as Jehovah had spoken" (Ex. 7:10-13).

THE PLAGUES. Then followed the ten great plagues which the Lord brought into Egypt. (1) Turning all the surface water into blood (Ex. 7:19-25); (2) frogs (Ex. 8:1-7); (3) lice (Ex. 8:16-19); (4) flies (Ex. 8:20-24); (5) death of domestic animals from murrain (Ex. 9:1-7); (6) boils on man and beast (Ex. 9:8-12); (7) hail (Ex. 9:17-35); (8) locusts Ex. 10:1-20); (9) darkness (Ex. 10:21-29); (10) death of the firstborn (Ex. 11:4-10; 12:29, 30).

PREPARATION FOR THE JOURNEY. In Midian God said to Moses: "I will give this people favor in the sight of the Egyptians: and it shall come to pass, that, when ye go, ye shall not be empty: but every woman shall ask of her neighbor, and of her that sojourneth in her house, jewels of silver, and jewels of gold, and raiment: and ye shall put them upon your sons, and upon your daughters; and ye shall despoil the Egyptians" (Ex. 3: 21, 22). Just before the final plague. God said to Moses: "Speak now in the ears of the people, and let them ask every man of his neighbor, and every woman of her neighbor, jewels of silver, and jewels of gold. And Jehovah gave the people favor in the sight of the Egyptians. Moreover the man Moses was very great in the land of Egypt, in the sight of Pharaoh's servants, and in the sight of the people" (Ex. 11:2, 3). The people followed these instructions; "and Jehovah gave the people favor in the sight of the Egyptians, so that they let them have what they asked. And they despoiled the Egyptians" (Ex. 12:35, 36).

THE PASSOVER

"And Jehovah spake unto Moses and Aaron in the land of Egypt, saying, This month shall be unto you the beginning of months: it shall be the first month of the year to you. Speak ye unto all the congregation of Israel, saying, In the tenth day of this month they shall take to them every man a lamb, according to their fathers' houses, a lamb for a household: and if the household be too little for a lamb, then shall he and his neighbor next unto his house take one according to the number of the souls; according to every man's eating ye shall make your count for the lamb. Your lamb shall be without blemish, a male a year old: ye shall take it from the sheep, or from the goats: and ye shall keep it until the fourteenth day of the same month; and the whole assembly of the congregation of Israel shall kill it at even. And they shall take of the blood, and put it on the two side-posts and on the lintel, upon the houses wherein they shall eat it. And they shall eat the flesh in that night, roast with fire, and unleaven bread; with bitter herbs they shall eat it. Eat not of it raw, nor boiled at all with water, but roast with fire; its head with its legs and with the inwards thereof. And ye shall let nothing of it remain until the morning; but that which remaineth of it until the morning ye shall burn with fire. And thus shall ye eat it: with your loins girded, your shoes upon your feet, and your staff in your hand; and ye shall eat it in haste: it is Jehovah's passover. For I will go through the land of Egypt in that night, and will smite all the firstborn in the land of Egypt, both man and beast; and against all the gods of Egypt I will execute judgments: I am Jehovah. And the blood shall be to you for a token upon the houses where ye are: and when I see the blood, I will pass over you, and there shall be no plague upon you to destroy you, when I smite the land of Egypt" (Ex. 12: 1-13).

THE DEPARTURE.

"And is came to pass at midnight, that Jehovah smote all the firstborn in the land of Egypt, from the firstborn of Pharaoh that sat upon his throne unto the firstborn of the captive that was in the dungeon; and all the firstborn of cattle. And Pharaoh rose up in the night, he, and all his servants, and all the Egyptians; and there was a great cry in Egypt; for there was not a house where there was not one dead. And he called for Moses and Aaron by night, and said, Rise up, get you forth from among my people, both ye and the children of Israel; and go, serve Jehovah, as ye have said. Take both your flocks and your herds, as ye have said, and be gone; and bless me also. And the Egyptians were urgent upon the people, to send them out of the land in haste; for they said, We are all dead men. And the people took their dough before it was leavened, their kneading-throughs being bound up in their clothes upon their shoulders" (Ex. 12:29-34). "And the children of Israel journeyed from Rameses to Succoth, about six hundred thousand on foot that were men, besides children. And a mixed multitude went up also with them" (Ex. 12:37, 38).

"And it came to pass, when Pharaoh had let the people go, that God led them not by the way of the land of the Philistines, although that was near; for God said, Lest peradventure the people repent when they see war, and they return to Egypt; but God led the people about, by the way of the wilderness by the Red Sea: and the children of Israel went up armed out of the land of Egypt. And Moses took the bones of Joseph with him. ..... And they took their journey from Succoth, and encamped in Etham, in the edge of the wilderness. And Jehovah went before them by day in a pillar of cloud, to lead them the way, and by night in a pillar of fire, to give them light; that they might go by day and by night: the pillar of cloud by day, and pillar of fire by night, departed not from before the people" (Ex. 13: 17-22).

PHARAOH AND HIS ARMY FOLLOW.

"And Jehovah spake unto Moses, saying, Speak unto the children of Israel, that they turn back and encamp before Pi-hahiroth, between Migdol and the sea, before Baal-zephon: over against it shall ye encamp by the sea" (Ex. 14:1, 2). And Pharaoh said: "What is this that we have done, that we have let Israel go from serving us? And he made ready his chariot, and took his people with him: and he took six hundred chosen chariots, and all the chariots of Egypt, and captains over all of them... And the Egyptians pursued after them, all the horses and chariots of Pharaoh, and his horsemen, and his army, and overtook them encamping by the sea" (Ex. 14:5-9).

WATERS DIVIDE—ISRAEL SAVED.

At sight of the Egyptians the Hebrews were filled with fear, and cried unto Jehovah, and complained against Moses: "For it were better for us to serve the Egyptians, than that we should die in the wilderness" (see Ex. 14:10-12). They had gone as far as Jehovah had directed; nothing more could be done till Jehovah spoke. Moses, with full confidence in God said: "Stand still, and see the salvation of Jehovah, which he will work for you today." "And Jehovah said unto Moses, Wherefore criest thou unto me? Speak unto the children of Israel, that they go forward. And lift thou up thy rod, and stretch out thy hand over the sea, and divide it; and the children of Israel shall go into the midst of the sea on dry ground" (Ex. 14:15, 16).

As the Hebrews moved toward the opening in the Red Sea, the pillar of fire moved back to their rear, so as to shut them off from the view of the Egyptians, and they crossed the sea on dry ground, the waters being a wall on either side of them. The Egyptians were pressing hard upon them—following them through the sea.

Having crossed the sea, at the command of Jehovah, Moses stretched his hand over the sea, the sea returned to its strength, and the Egyptians were drowned. "Thus Jehovah saved Israel that day out of the hands of the Egyptians" (Ex. 14:30). "Thus," in the manner described, "Jehovah saved Israel." True, they had to do everything Jehovah commanded, but their salvation was none the less of Jehovah. They were saved the day they crossed the Red Sea—that day Jehovah saved them. Be it remembered: They were baptized the day they crossed the sea (see I Cor. 10:1, 2).

Being delivered from bondage, saved from the hands of the Egyptians, they sang the songs of deliverance (see Ex. 15).

* * *

TOPICS FOR INVESTIGATION AND DISCUSSION.

God's Providence as Illustrated in the Child Moses.
Moses' Choice (Heb. 11:24-26).
Signs and Their Purpose.
The Character of Pharaoh.
The Feast of the Passover.

* * *

QUESTIONS

1. By what names were Jacob's descendants called?
2. To whom was the name "Hebrew" first applied?
3. Who was first called "Israel," and when?
4. Where does the word "Jew" first occur in the Bible?
5. To whom was it applied?
6. What constituted a tribe of Israel?
7. What happened to Israel after the death of Joseph?
8. Describe the severity of their bondage.
9. What measures were adopted to prevent their increase?
10. Why prevent their increase?
11. Of what tribe was Moses?
12. Tell how he came into the hands of Pharaoh's daughter and how his mother became his nurse.

DELIVERANCE OF HEBREWS 41

13. What of his education and training?
14. How came Moses to leave Egypt?
15. Where did he go?
16. What was his age at this time?
17. With whom did he sojourn?
18. How long did he remain in Midian?
19. What was his occupation?
20. Where did an angel appear to him?
21. Tell what took place at this appearance.
22. On what mission did God propose to send him?
23. What is implied in Moses' first objection?
24. What change does this indicate had taken place in his character since he killed the Egyptian in his first attempt to deliver his brethren?
25. What was his second objection to going?
26. What means did God give Moses to cause his brethren to believe?
27. What was Moses' third objection?
28. Why was God's anger kindled, and what did he say?
29. What was to be Aaron's part?
30. Whom did Moses and Aaron first gather together?
31. What then did they say to Pharaoh?
32. What was Pharaoh's reply?
33. What do you think of such a challenge?
34. What does it indicate as to Pharaoh's character?
35. Of what did Pharaoh accuse Moses and Aaron?
36. What then did he command the taskmasters?
37. Tell what occurred at their second visit to Pharaoh.
38. Name the ten plagues.
39. Tell how they collected so much silver, gold, and raiment.
40. What were they commanded to do on the tenth day of the first month?
41. What should a small household do?
42. What kind of a lamb?
43. How long was the lamb to be kept up?
44. What do with the blood?
45. How was the lamb to be cooked?
46. With what were they to eat it?
47. How were they to eat it?
48. What occurred at midnight?
49. What houses did the destroying angel pass over?
50. What did Pharaoh do?
51. Why was he so urgent that Israel go?

52. How many Israelites went?
53. Did any others go?
54. From what place did they depart?
55. Whose bones did they carry? (see Acts 7:15, 16).
56. Why did not God lead them through the land of the Philistines?
57. Tell how they were guided in their journey?
58. What did Pharaoh do?
59. What is said of his equipment?
60. Where did they overtake Israel?
61. How did the sight of them affect Israel?
62. What did Moses command?
63. What did God command?
64. How were the waters of the Red Sea parted?
65. What is said of the pillar of fire?
66. Tell how the Egyptians were destroyed.
67. How did the Lord save Israel from the Egyptians?
68. When did Israel sing the song of deliverance?

DELIVERANCE FROM SIN.

AN ANALOGY. Many good Bible students hold to the idea that the bondage of the Israelites in Egypt is a type of our bondage in sin, their deliverance a type of our deliverance, their baptism unto Moses in the cloud and sea a type of our baptism into Christ, their journey through the wilderness a type of the Christian life, their crossing the Jordan a type of death, and Canaan a type of our heavenly home. But if this is a type, there are important points where the type and the antitype fail to agree. However, there is a striking analogy between the two. On this analogy, this resemblance, the present lesson is constructed.

ISRAEL'S BONDAGE. Had the Israelites been free and prosperous in Egypt, had they not been reduced by cruel and oppressive bondage, they never would have desired to leave that land; but they were reduced to the cruelest of bondage, and their lives became bitter.

OUR BONDAGE. "Every one that committeth sin is the bondservant of sin" (John 8:34). "Know ye not, that to whom ye present yourselves as servants unto obedience, his servants ye are whom ye obey; whether of sin unto death, or of obedience unto righteousness?" (Rom. 6:16). Satan is a cruel taskmaster; he promises us just enough of pleasure to lure us on to ruin in this life and the life to come. "The wages of sin is death." If we would only think seriously about sin and its awful consequences, it would become an unbearable burden, and there would spring up in our hearts a longing for freedom from its galling yoke of cruel bondage. Jesus invites those who are weary of sin, those upon whom sin rests as a heavy burden, to come to him for rest, for freedom.

MOSES THEIR DELIVERER. Being moved with compassion for the Israelites on account of their sufferings, God appeared to Moses and said: "And now, behold, the cry of the children of Israel is come unto me: moreover I have seen the oppression wherewith the Egyptians oppress them. Come now therefore, and I will send thee unto Pharaoh, that thou mayest bring forth my people the children of Israel out of Egypt" (Ex. 3:9, 10). Stephen said: "This Moses whom they refused, saying, Who made thee a ruler and a judge? him hath God sent to be both a ruler and a deliverer with the hand of the angel that appeared to him in the bush" (Acts 7:35).

CHRIST OUR DELIVERER. "Jehovah thy God will raise up unto thee a prophet from the midst of thee, of thy brethren, like unto me; unto him ye shall hearken.... I will raise them up a prophet from among their brethren, like unto thee; and I will put my words in his mouth, and he shall speak unto them all that I shall command him. And it shall come to pass, that whosoever will not hearken unto my words which he shall speak in my name, I will require it of him" (Deut. 18:15-19). "For God so loved the world, that he gave his only begotten Son, that whosoever believeth on him should not perish, but have eternal life. For God sent not the Son into the world to judge the world; but that the world should be saved through him" (John 3:16, 17). "If therefore the Son shall make you free, ye shall be free indeed" (John 8:36).

Jesus took on himself the nature of man "that through death he might bring to naught him that had the power of death, that is, the devil; and might deliver all them who through fear of death were all their lifetime subject to bondage" (Heb. 2:14, 15).

The world to-day is burdened with dishonesty, immorality, robbery, murder—with sins of every kind; in Jesus alone is there hope of deliverance.

FAITH NECESSARY THEN. Moses, realizing that unless the Israelites believed him he could do nothing, said: "But, behold, they will not believe me, nor hearken unto my voice; for they will say, Jehovah hath not appeared unto thee" (Ex. 4:1).

WE MUST BELIEVE. "Except ye believe that I am he ye shall die in your sins" (John 8:24). "He that disbelieveth shall be condemned" (Mark 16:16). "Without faith it is impossible to be well-pleasing unto him; for he that cometh to God must believe that he is, and that he is a rewarder of them that seek after him" (Heb. 11:6).

HOW THEIR FAITH CAME. "And Aaron spake all the words which Jehovah had spoken unto Moses, and did the signs in the sight of the people. And the people believed" (Ex. 4:30, 31).

HOW FAITH IS PRODUCED. "Many other signs therefore did Jesus in the presence of the disciples, which are not written in this book: but these are written that ye may believe that Jesus is the Christ, the Son of God; and that believing ye may have life in his name" (John 20:30, 31). "And it came to pass in Iconium that they entered together into the synagogue of the Jews, and so spake that a great multitude both of the Jews and of Greeks believed" (Acts 14:1). "So belief cometh of hearing, and hearing by the word of Christ" (Rom. 10:17).

PURPOSE OF MIRACLES OF MOSES. When Moses objected to making an effort to lead Israel out of bondage because the people would say, "Jehovah hath not appeared to thee," God gave him signs to perform in their presence to show them that God was with him (see Ex. 4:1-9, 29-31). The signs did not produce faith, nor enlighten them as to the nature of the mission of Moses, but they were God's guaranty that the message delivered by Moses was true.

SIGNS IN THE CHRISTIAN DISPENSATION. "And they went forth, and preached everywhere, the Lord working with them, and confirming the word by the signs that followed" (Mark 16:20). "How shall we escape, if we neglect so great a salvation? which having at the first been spoken through the Lord was confirmed unto us by them that heard; God also bearing witness with them, both by signs and wonders, and by manifold powers, and by gifts of the Holy Spirit, according to his own will" (Heb. 2:3, 4). Nicodemus had the correct idea of signs: "Rabbi, we know that thou art a teacher come from God; for no one can do these signs that thou doest, except God be with him" (John 3:2).

REPENTANCE. They had to make up their mind to forsake Egypt and follow Moses. We must determine to forsake sin and follow Christ. There must be such a change in our mind and heart as will result in a reformation of life. "Except ye repent, ye shall all likewise perish" (Luke 13:5).

DELIVERANCE CONDITIONAL. God could have taken up the whole Jewish nation and carried them to Canaan, just as he took Enoch to heaven; but he did not choose to do so. He made it possible for them to leave Egypt, and guided them and provided for their needs on the way, but they had to cooperate with him in their deliverance. Their deliverance was not unconditional—they had to do what they could.

OUR DELIVERANCE CONDITIONAL. It is not a question of what God can do, but of what he proposes to do. "Not every one that saith unto me, Lord, Lord, shall enter into the kingdom of heaven; but he that doeth the will of my Father who is in heaven" (Matt. 7:21). God will render to every man according to his works; eternal life to those who seek for glory and honor and incorruption, tribulation and anguish to those who obey not the truth (Rom. 2:6-11). Jesus Christ became the author of eternal salvation to all who obey him (Heb. 5:8). Follow Jesus and live in freedom, or refuse and die in bondage to Satan.

BAPTIZED UNTO MOSES. "For I would not, brethren, have you ignorant, that our fathers were all under the cloud, and all passed through the sea; and were all baptized unto (Greek, *into*) Moses in the cloud and in the sea" (I Cor. 10:1, 2). Though they were following Moses before they were baptized, they were yet the property, the unwilling slaves, of Pharaoh, and were not completely under the undisputed leadership of Moses till their former owners were destroyed in the Red Sea. Here they passed from the ownership of the Egyptians into the leadership of Moses—baptized into Moses, into his leadership.

They were baptized in the cloud and in the sea—it took both elements to constitute their baptism. Any theory concerning their baptism that leaves out either element is wrong. It is contended by some that they were baptized by the rain. But the text relied upon to support this theory (Ps. 68:8) does not say the rain fell while they were crossing the sea. The rain came after they crossed—at Mount Sinai. But if it could be shown that the rain fell as they were crossing the sea, it is certain that it did not constitute their baptism. The rain theory is wrong; for if they were baptized in the rain, the sea had nothing to do with their baptism. The waters stood upright as a wall on either side frozen, and the cloud hid them from the view of the Egyptians. They were thus buried, immersed, in the cloud and in the sea.

BAPTIZED INTO CHRIST. "Or are ye ignorant that all we who were baptized into Christ Jesus were baptized into his death?" (Rom. 6:3). Baptism is the dividing line between the world and the church, between servitude to sin and freedom in Christ. "He that believeth and is baptized shall be saved" (Mark 16:16). "Repent ye and be baptized every one of you in the name of Jesus Christ unto the remission of your sins; and ye shall receive the gift of the Holy Spirit" (Acts 2:38). "And now why tarriest thou? arise, and be baptized, and wash away thy sins, calling on his name" (Acts 22:16).

SAVED FROM BONDAGE. "Thus Jehovah saved Israel that day out of the hand of the Egyptians" (Ex. 14:30). "Thus," in the manner described, "the Lord saved Israel." The Lord saved them by opening up the way and destroying their enemies, and they saved themselves by going forward as God commanded them.

SAVED FROM SIN. Jesus is our Savior, and there is none other that can save (Acts 4:12). He prepared the way for us to be saved and forgives our sins, and we save ourselves by accepting salvation on the conditions laid down. After the way had been pointed out on the great Pentecost, Peter exhorted them: "Save yourselves."

HOW THEY WERE GUIDED. "And Jehovah went before them by day in a pillar of cloud, to lead them the way, and by night in a pillar of fire, to give them light; that they might go by day and by night: the pillar of cloud by day, and the pillar of fire by night, departed not from before the people" (Ex. 13:21, 22). "And when the cloud was taken up from over the tabernacle, the children of Israel went onward throughout all their journeys: but if the cloud was not taken up, then they journeyed not till the day that it was taken up" (Ex. 40:36, 37).

OUR GUIDE. "Then Jesus said unto his disciples, If any man would come after me, let him deny himself, and take up his cross, and follow me" (Matt. 16:24; see also Mark 8:34; Luke 9:23). "Again therefore Jesus spake unto them, saying, I am the light of the world:

he that followeth me shall not walk in the darkness, but shall have the light of life" (John 8:12). "Christ also suffered for you, leaving you an example, that ye should follow his steps" (I Peter 2:21). We follow Christ by imitating his example and obeying his commands. "Thy word is a lamp unto my feet, and light unto my path" (Ps. 119:105). Our loyalty must not be divided —we must follow him with the whole heart. To do so we must repudiate human creeds and all the doctrines of men.

THEIR FOOD. God supplied them with food during their journey through the wilderness. "And it came to pass at even, that the quails came up, and covered the camp: and in the morning the dew lay round about the camp. And when the dew that lay was gone up, behold, upon the face of the wilderness a small round thing, small as the hoar-frost on the ground..... And Moses said unto them, It is the bread which Jehovah hath given you to eat" (Ex. 16:13-15). "And the house of Israel called the name thereof Manna: and it was like coriander seed, white; and the taste of it was like wafers made with honey" (Ex. 16:31). "And the children of Israel did eat the manna forty years, until they came to a land inhabited; they did eat the manna, until they came unto the borders of the land of Canaan" (Ex. 16:35).

OUR SPIRITUAL FOOD. "Jesus therefore said unto them, Verily, verily, I say unto you, It was not Moses that gave you the bread out of heaven; but my Father giveth you the true bread out of heaven. For the bread of God is that which cometh down out of heaven, and giveth life unto the world. They said therefore unto him, Lord, evermore give us this bread. Jesus said unto them, I am the bread of life: he that cometh to me shall not hunger, and he that believeth on me shall never thirst" (John 6:32-35). "Your fathers ate the manna in the wilderness, and they died. This is the bread which cometh down out of heaven, that a man may eat thereof and not die. I am the living bread which came down out of heaven: if any man eat of this bread, he shall live for ever: yea and the bread which I will give is my flesh, for the life of the world" (John 6:49-51).

The Israelites drank from the rock that followed them, and that rock was Christ (I Cor. 10:4). That rock was a type of Christ. "Except ye eat the flesh of the Son of man and drink his blood, ye have no life in yourselves. He that eateth my flesh and drinketh my blood hath eternal life; and I will raise him up at the last day. For my flesh is meat indeed, and my blood is drink indeed" (John 6:53-55). We eat his flesh and drink his blood—that is, we appropriate the benefits of both—by studying and doing his will. "As newborn babes, long for the spiritual milk which is without guile, that ye may grow thereby unto salvation; if ye have tasted that the Lord is gracious" (I Peter 2:2, 3). Spiritual life will perish without spiritual food. All over this land Christians are perishing for lack of food and drink. "My people perish for lack of knowledge." Many have a name to live, but are dead.

THEIRS A JOURNEY OF TRUST. They depended not on themselves for guidance. God, through Moses, was their teacher, and by the cloud and the pillar of fire he led them in their journey.

OURS A LIFE OF TRUST. "It is not in man that walketh to direct his steps." No one knows the way of life and salvation, only as it is revealed to him. Many of the Israelites fell through unbelief, and we are exhorted to take heed lest we fall after the same example of unbelief (Heb. 4:11). Unbelief most commonly manifests itself in the making of human creeds and in the various schemes for which no authority can be found in the New Testament. A lack of confidence in the wisdom and goodness of God is alone responsible for all the new fads and schemes of present-day religionists.

MANY FELL. "Howbeit with most of them God was not well pleased: for they were overthrown in the wilderness" (I Cor. 10:5). "And Jehovah spake unto Moses and unto Aaron, saying, How long shall I bear with this evil congregation, that murmur against me? ..... As I live, saith Jehovah, ... your dead bodies shall fall in this wilderness; and all that were numbered of you, according to your whole number, from twenty years old and upward, that have murmured against me, surely ye shall not come into the land, concerning which I sware that I would make you dwell therein, save Caleb the son of Jephunneh, and Joshua the son of Nun. But your little ones, that ye said should be a prey, them will I bring in" (Num. 14:26-31).

CAN WE FALL? "Now these things were our examples, to the intent we should not lust after evil things, as they also lusted" (I Cor. 10:6). "Now these things happened unto them by way of example; and they were written for our admonition, upon whom the ends of the ages are come. Wherefore let him that thinketh he standeth take heed lest he fall" (I Cor. 10:11, 12). If man cannot fall, then this admonition is entirely useless.

THE RIVER JORDAN. Before the Israelites could dwell in the promised land of Canaan, they had to cross the river Jordan. They were miraculously aided in crossing Jordan, as they were in crossing the Red Sea (see Josh. 3).

DEATH. Before we reach our promised inheritance we must pass through death. Jordan has come to be a symbol of death, and we sing that soul-stirring hymn:

> On Jordan's stormy banks I stand,
> And cast a wishful eye,
> To Canaan's fair and happy land,
> Where my possessions lie.

O, the transporting, rapturous scene
    That rises to my sight!
Sweet fields arrayed in living green,
    And rivers of delight!

All o'er these wide-extended plains
    Shines one eternal day,
There God, the Sun, forever reigns,
    And scatters night away.

When shall I reach that happy place,
    And be forever blest?
When shall I see my Father's face,
    And in his bosom rest?

Fill'd with delight, my raptur'd soul
    Would here no longer stay;
Though Jordan's waves around me roll,
    Fearless I'd launch away.

* * *

TOPICS FOR INVESTIGATION AND DISCUSSION.

The Spies and Their Report (Num. 13, 14).

Korah's Rebellion and the People's Complaint (Num. 16).

The Fiery Serpents (Num. 21:4-9).

Balaam (Num. 22, 23, 24).

The Death of Moses, and Why He Did Not Enter Canaan.

* * *

QUESTIONS

1. Is the deliverance of Israel a type of our deliverance from sin? Give reason for your answer.
2. Give the meaning of the word "analogy."
3. Describe the severity of Israel's bondage.
4. To what are sinners in bondage?
5. What brought about this bondage?
6. Give some of the consequences of this bondage.
7. Who are invited to escape this bondage?
8. What moved God to deliver Israel?

DELIVERANCE FROM SIN

9. Who was sent to deliver them?
10. Who is our Deliverer?
11. Wherein is he like unto Moses?
12. What moved God to send this Deliverer?
13. Why did Jesus take on himself the nature of man?
14. Why did Israel have to believe?
15. What degree of faith was necessary?
16. Discuss the need of faith now.
17. How was their faith produced?
18. How does faith come now?
19. Discuss the purpose of signs.
20. What of repentance?
21. What did they do toward their own deliverance?
22. Can we do anything in our deliverance?
23. When were they freed from the Egyptians?
24. Describe their baptism.
25. Prove that their baptism was not sprinkling by midst from the walls of water, nor by rain.
26. Prove that in baptism we are freed from sin.
27. How did Jehovah save Israel?
28. How did they save themselves?
29. How may we save ourselves?
30. How were the Israelites guided?
31. Who is our guide?
32. Give some quotations of scripture on this point.
33. What was their food?
34. Who gave them that food?
35. What is our food and drink?
36. How may we take this food and drink?
37. What is spiritual milk?
38. Why do Christians perish?
39. Show why they needed guidance and why we do. Why do men invent things in religion?
40. How many men over twenty years old came out of Egypt?
41. How many of these fell in the wilderness?
42. Why did they fall in the wilderness?
43. What is the lesson to us? Can we fall?
44. Describe their crossing the Jordan.
45. Why has the river Jordan became a symbol of death?
46. Why did Moses fail to enter Canaan?

THE TEN COMMANDMENTS.

LESSON TEXT: Ex. 20:1-17.
TIME: B. C. 1491.
PLACE: Mount Sinai.
MEMORY VERSES: Gal. 3:23-25.

MOUNT SINAI. It is not known that the mountain now known as Mount Sinai is the identical mountain from which the Ten Commandments were given. It is about midway between the Gulf of Suez and Akabah. It is a rock-ribbed mountain, composed largely of granite, about two miles long and a mile wide. It is about 7,500 feet above sea level. The descendants of Abraham, the Israelites, were in Egypt four hundred and thirty years (Gal. 3:17). Fifty days after they crossed the Red Sea they reached Mount Sinai, where they received the Ten Commandments. This was about twenty-five hundred years after Adam sinned and was cast out of the garden.

MORAL LAWS

Moral laws are laws which have to do with man's relationship to his fellows and his moral life. In this class are "Thou shalt not kill," "steal," "lie," etc. Had Jehovah never given a law covering these and kindred matters, it would have been wrong to steal, kill, etc. Such laws are right within themselves.

POSITIVE LAWS.

Positive laws are laws which God has enacted and which depend wholly on Jehovah's authority to make them right. Among such laws is the one relating to the passover (Ex. 12), purifying (Num. 19), and kindred laws. They were right—to be observed because God commanded them. Had he not commanded them, there would have been no ground for their observance.

TO WHOM WERE THE TEN COMMANDMENTS GIVEN?

When Jehovah called Abraham, he bade him leave his relatives and go to a land to be shown him. The descendants of Abraham became a special people unto Jehovah (Deut. 7:6; 14:2); and to these people the Ten Commandments were given, as is plainly stated in the lesson text:

Ex. 20:1, 2. "And God spake all these words, saying, I am Jehovah thy God, who brought thee out of the land of Egypt, out of the house of bondage." Then follows the Ten Commandments. Let it be remembered that these words were addressed to the descendants of Abraham. Not a Gentile was in the number. Gentiles were never slaves in Egypt.

THE TEN COMMANDMENTS

I. "Thou shalt have no other gods before me." Jehovah is a person, not an influence, and as such reveals himself to man. No object or person is comparable to him. That which man worships he will come in time to resemble, and the object of worship becomes your god.

From bondage Jehovah delivered the Israelites; no other could have delivered them. He is Creator, Preserver, Deliverer. This commandment forbids idolatry, and it should be remembered you do not have to erect an image of wood or stone to have an idol. For centuries the Jews had been in Egypt, where there were idols on every hand, and were on their way to Canaan, where the land was filled with idols. We are influenced by our environments.

II. "Thou shalt not make unto thee a graven image,

nor any likeness of anything that is in heaven above, or that is in the earth beneath, or that is in the water under the earth: thou shalt not bow down thyself unto them, nor serve them; for I Jehovah thy God am a jealous God, visiting the iniquity of the fathers upon the children, upon the third and upon the fourth generation of them that hate me, and showing loving-kindness unto thousands of them that love me and keep my commandments."

GRAVEN IMAGES. This does not forbid paintings, sculpture, etc., as is evidenced by Jehovah's directing that cherubims be placed in the most holy place (Ex. 25:17-22). The prohibition is against making images to be worshiped. The first images made and worshiped were most likely not regarded as gods, but only as representatives of gods. This Jehovah forbids.

NOR SERVE THEM. Soon after giving this commandment the people made a golden calf, worshiped it, made sacrifices to it (Ex. 32). They broke the second commandment.

JEALOUS GOD. It is not good for any people to worship a being, or image, inferior to Jehovah. The effect is debasing. Our homage must be paid one who is worthy of our adoration and praise.

VISITING INIQUITY. You know something of the law of heredity. There are diseases entailed in the natural body (Ex. 34:7; Jer. 32:18). Surely you know the result of sin may not end with you. The abuse of your body may be seen in your offspring. A vicious family is a hindrance to the country. Though one may have had vicious parents, each individual has within himself the making of a character which will adorn society and honor Jehovah.

THIRD AND FOURTH GENERATION. It should be remembered that this is no more than a weakened condition of the body entailed on us, and for such conditions we are not condemned (Ezek. 18:20).

SHOWING MERCY. Often you hear quoted: "I will have mercy on whom I have mercy." Certainly, but on whom does he have mercy? "He that covereth his transgressions shall not prosper; but whoso confesseth and forsaketh them shall obtain mercy" (Prov. 28:13).

III. "Thou shalt not take the name of Jehovah thy God in vain; for Jehovah will not hold him guiltless that taketh his name in vain." All profanity is forbidden. To carelessly and irreverently use his name, or to use his name as a byword, is sinful. Swearing never benefited the swearer nor the one who hears the oath. You cannot give one reason for swearing. Good people lose respect for the man who swears—they do not wish their children to associate with such. Profanity is a characteristic of the low—those of the slums. The most vile oaths I ever heard were in the asylum. Those who swear never use the name of their mother, wife, or sweetheart—they never use the name of one they love in a profane expression. Do you love God? Do you swear in the presence of your wife, your mother, the minister of your church, ladies? You are always in the presence of Jehovah. Is it even gentlemanly to swear? Most drunken men swear, and the more drunken the more profane his oaths. "Don't shoot your arrow into the dark; you may hit your best friend." Be careful; never use profane language; you may wound your best friend.

IV. "Remember the sabbath day, to keep it holy. Six days shalt thou labor, and do all thy work; but the seventh day is a sabbath unto Jehovah thy God: in it thou shalt not do any work, thou, nor thy son, nor thy daughter, nor thy manservant, nor thy maidservant, nor thy cattle, nor thy stranger that is within thy gates: for in six days Jehovah made heaven and earth, the sea, and all that in them is, and rested the seventh day: wherefore Jehovah blessed the sabbath day and hallowed it."

The first mention of the Sabbath is in the sixteenth chapter of Exodus, when manna was given. There is no proof that it existed as a formal institution before the time of Moses. The Jews were commanded to do all their labor within six days, and to rest on the seventh day. They were not allowed to do any kind of work on the Sabbath day (Ex. 31:14). They were not allowed to pick up sticks on the Sabbath (Num. 15:32-35), nor were they allowed to make a fire (Ex. 35:3). In a subsequent volume we will discuss at length the Sabbath, and why Christians do not "keep it."

V. "Honor thy father and thy mother, that thy days may be long in the land which Jehovah thy God giveth thee." Some of the savages, when their parents became old and infirm—nonproductive members of society—put them to death or abandoned them. The mother amongst the heathens was an inferior person, and when the husband died she was required to obey the oldest son.

HONOR. Honor means more than to obey. Though you reach maturity, and have a home of your own, you must always honor your parents. By your conduct you reflect honor or discredit on your parents. To do or say things you would not have them know is to dishonor them. Do not wait until your parents are dead, and then engage in bitter lamentations because you failed to honor them.

THAT THY DAYS MAY BE LONG. The child who disregards filial authority, failing to honor parents, will develop into a man who will disregard the law of State and society; he becomes an evildoer, and comes to death by disease resulting from a profligate life or dies by the hands of the executor of the law.

VI. "Thou shalt not kill." ("Thou shalt do no murder"—R. V). There is a clear distinction between killing and murder. In Old Testament times some people were, by the authority of Jehovah, put to death because of crimes they committed. Animals were killed in sacrifice to him. Murder is always wrong. Murder is killing through hatred, through malice or greed for gain. Suicide is murder, whether it is performed in a moment or is the result of vicious habits—intemperance.

VII. "Thou shalt not commit adultery." Some are confused over adultery and fornication. Adultery is unlawful intercourse with the wife of another. Fornication is a broader term and embraces the sin of adultery, as well as unlawful intercourse between those who are not married. The family is the basis of the home, the church, and the State. If the family relationship is not maintained, chaos will follow in the home as well as in the nation, and the world will be filled with illegitimate and vicious children. He who loves the woman to whom he is married will not prostitute his body.

VIII. "Thou shalt not steal." Theft is depriving one of that which rightly belongs to him, whether it be by stealth or by taking advantage of the ignorance or inexperience of some one in trade. Stealing is possible in every field of activity. Some steal time from those who employ them. Some students steal when taking an examination. He who contracts debts when he has no money with which to meet his obligations, and no prospect for earning that money, is a thief.

IX. "Thou shalt not bear false witness against thy neighbor." All courts recognize the enormity of the sin of false swearing, and punish it severely. There are many ways in which one can bear false witness: "(1) In saying about a man what we know to be untrue; (2) in keeping silent when others say it; (3) in passing it on to others, by word of mouth or in print; (4) in refusing to say for a man what we can; (5) in making statements about others we do not know to be true; (6) in speaking half-truths, when we should tell the whole truth; (7) by twisting the truth by giving the wrong emphasis."—Peloubet. You may bear false witness by acting a hypocrite, by placing on goods false labels. Moses refused to be called the son of Pharaoh's daughter. He was thought to be such by the masses of the people; but Moses knew better, and he refused to be silent when he knew his very silence contributed to the deception being practiced.

X. "Thou shalt not covet." A desire for more than you now possess may be a healthy ambition. You should make every dollar you can, honestly; at the same time you must not abuse yourself while doing this. I think there has never been a time in the history of humanity when money could be so advantageously used in blessing humanity as now. Remember, you are not only responsible for making money, but for how you spend it as well.

COVETOUSNESS. Covetousness is an inordinate desire to possess that which belongs to another—it is the mother of theft. Aside from the law of Jehovah, there is not a system of laws under heaven which forbids covetousness.

THE TEN COMMANDMENTS—THE OLD COVENANT.

"Behold, the days come, saith Jehovah, that I will make a new covenant with the house of Israel, and with the house of Judah: not according to the covenant that I made with their fathers in the day that I took them by the hand to bring them out of the land of Egypt; which my covenant they brake, although I was a husband unto them, saith Jehovah. But this is the covenant that I will make with the house of Israel after those days, saith Jehovah: I will put my law in their inward parts, and in their heart will I write it; and I will be their God, and they shall be my people. And they shall teach no more every man his neighbor, and every man his brother, saying, Know Jehovah; for they shall all know me, from the least of them unto the greatest of them, saith Jehovah: for I will forgive their iniquity, and their sin will I remember no more" (Jer. 31:31-34). (1) This covenant was made with Israel when they were brought from the land of Egypt—the Ten Commandments were then given. (2) A new covenant is promised, which is not to be like the old covenant.

THE COVENANT — EVEN TEN COMMANDMENTS. "And Jehovah spake unto you out of the midst of the fire: ye heard the voice of words, but ye saw no form; only ye heard a voice. And he declared unto you his covenant, which he commanded you to perform, even the Ten Commandments; and he wrote them upon two tables of stone" (Deut. 4:12, 13).

TABLES OF THE COVENANT. "When I was gone up into the mount to receive the tables of stone, even the tables of the covenant which Jehovah made with you, then I abode in the mount forty days and forty nights; I did neither eat bread nor drink water. And Jehovah delivered unto me the two tables of stone written with the finger of God; and on them was written according to all the words, which Jehovah spake unto you in the mount out of the midst of the fire in the day of the assembly. And it came to pass at the end of forty days and forty nights, that Jehovah gave me the two tables of stone, even the tables of the covenant" (Deut. 9:9-11).

WORDS OF THE COVENANT. "And he was there with Jehovah forty days and forty nights; he did neither eat bread, nor drink water. And he wrote upon the tables the words of the covenant, the Ten Commandments" (Ex. 34:28). That the Ten Commandments is the covenant that Jehovah made with them when they came from the land of Egypt cannot be successfully denied.

THE OLD COVENANT, THE TEN COMMANDMENTS, TAKEN AWAY. "But now hath he obtained a ministry the more excellent, by so much as he is also the mediator of a better covenant, which hath been enacted upon better promises. For if that first covenant had been faultless, then would no place have been sought for a second. For finding fault with them, he said, Behold the days come, saith the Lord, that I will make a new covenant with the house of Israel and with the house of Judah; not according to the covenant that I made with their fathers in the day that I took them by the hand to lead them forth out of the land of Egypt; for they continued not in my covenant, and I regarded them not, saith the Lord. For this is the covenant that I will make with the house of Israel after those days, saith the Lord; I will put my laws into their minds, and on their hearts also will I write them: and I will be to them a God, and they shall be to me a people: and they shall not teach every man his fellow-citizen, and every man his brother, saying, Know the Lord: for all shall know me, from the least to the greatest of them. For I will be merciful to their iniquities, and their sins will I remember no more. In that he saith a new covenant, he hath made the first old" (Heb. 8:6-13). Jesus is the mediator of a better covenant than the one made at Mount Siani. It is a covenant which is established upon better promises. The covenant from Mount Sinai is called the "old covenant." Christ is mediator of the "new covenant" (Heb. 9:15).

WRITTEN AND ENGRAVEN IN STONE. "And Moses turned, and went down from the mount, with the two tables of the testimony in his hand; tables that were written on both their sides; on the one side and on the other were they written. And the tables were the work of God, and the writing was the writing of God, graven upon the tables" (Ex. 32:15, 16). "And he gave unto Moses, when he had made an end of communing with him upon Mount Sinai, the two tables of the testimony, tables of stone, written with the finger of God" (Ex. 31:18).

THAT WHICH WAS ENGRAVEN IN STONE HAS BEEN DONE AWAY. Paul affirms that God had made them "ministers of a new covenant; not of the letter, but of the spirit: for the letter killeth, but the spirit giveth life. But if the ministration of death, written, and engraven on stones, came with glory, so that the children of Israel could not look steadfastly upon the face of Moses for the glory of his face; which glory was passing away: how shall not rather the ministration of the spirit be with glory? For if the ministration of condemnation hath glory, much rather doth the ministration of righteousness exceed in glory. For verily that which hath been made glorious hath not been made glorious in this respect, by reason of the glory that surpasseth. For if that which passeth away was glory, much more that which remaineth is in glory. Having therefore such a hope, we use great boldness of speech, and are not as Moses, who put a veil over his face, that the children of Israel should not look steadfastly on the end of that which was passing away: but their minds were hardened: for until this very day at the reading of the old covenant, the same veil remaineth, it not being revealed to them that it is done away in Christ" (II Cor. 3:6-14).

HOW LONG WAS THE LAW TO BE IN FORCE? "What then is the law? It was added because of transgressions, till the seed should come" (Gal. 3:19).

THE LAW A SCHOOLMASTER—TILL CHRIST CAME. "But before faith came, we were kept in ward under the law, shut up unto the faith which should afterwards be revealed. So that the law is become our tutor to bring us unto Christ, that we might be justified by faith. But now that faith is come, we are no longer under a tutor" (Gal. 3:23-25).

Do not become alarmed because the Ten Commandments have been repealed. Remember, a new covenant has been made. Texas was at one time a republic, with constitution and laws. The constitution and laws of the Republic of Texas are not binding in the State of Texas; but, as a State, Texas now has a constitution and laws.

In the new covenant which Jehovah has made we find nine of the points covered by the Ten Commandments are incorporated and enlarged on; and they are binding, not because they were in the old covenant, but because they are in the new.

HOW READS THE NEW.	THE TEN COMMANDMENTS.
"Turn from these vain things unto a living God, who made the heaven and the earth and the sea, and all that in them is" (Acts 14:15).	I. Thou shalt have no other gods before me.
Guard yourselves from idols.	II. Thou shalt not make unto thee a graven image.
"Swear not, neither by the heaven, nor by the earth, nor by any other oath" (James 5:12).	III. Thou shalt not take the name of Jehovah thy God in vain.
There is not a command in the new covenant to keep the Sabbath.	IV. Remember the sabbath day, to keep it holy.
"Children, obey your parents in the Lord: for this is right. Honor thy father and mother" (Eph. 6:1, 2).	V. Honor thy father and thy mother.
"Thou shalt not kill" (Rom. 13:9). "Whosoever hateth his brother is a murderer" (I John 3:15).	VI. Thou shalt not kill.

THE TEN COMMANDMENTS

"Know ye not that the unrighteous shall not inherit the kingdom of God? Be not deceived: neither fornicators, nor idolaters, nor adulterers" (I Cor. 6:9).

"Let him that stole steal no more" (Eph. 4:28).

"Lie not one to another" (Col. 3:9).

"Covetousness is idolatry" (Col. 3:5).

VII. Thou shalt not commit adultery.

VIII. Thou shalt not steal.

IX. Thou shalt not bear false witness.

X. Thou shalt not covet.

There is not a command in all the New Testament to keep the Sabbath day holy. Gentiles were never commanded to keep the Sabbath day.

In a later volume we will discuss the Sabbath and the Lord's day.

The student should review the lesson on "The Covenants," in Vol. I. of "Sound Doctrine."

* * *

TOPICS FOR INVESTIGATION AND DISCUSSION.

1. Positive and Moral Laws.
2. Were the Ten Commandments a Perfect Law?
3. Law and Grace.
4. How is the New Covenant Written in the Heart?
5. Moses.

* * *

QUESTIONS

1. In what country is Mount Sinai?
2. From what mountain were the Ten Commandments given?
3. How long after creation before the Ten Commandments were given?
4. How long were the Israelites in bondage?
5. Give the history of why they were in bondage.

SOUND DOCTRINE

6. How long after they crossed the Red Sea before the giving of the Ten Commandments?
7. What is meant in the lesson by "moral" commandments?
8. What is meant in the lesson by "positive" commandments?
9. To whom were the Ten Commandments given?
10. Why given to the Israelites?
11. Show that the Ten Commandments were not given to the Gentiles.
12. What was the first commandment?
13. What is an idol?
14. What the first idol made by Israel after leaving Egypt?
15. How long after they crossed the Red Sea?
16. Does prostituting our bodies affect our offspring?
17. Do we inherit sin?
18. To whom is mercy shown?
19. How may one take the name of God in vain?
20. Why do people swear?
21. What was the fourth commandment?
22. When was the Sabbath first mentioned?
23. What day was the Sabbath?
24. Do people "keep" the Sabbath now?
25. Can there be a law without a penalty?
26. What was done to those who made fires or picked up sticks on the Sabbath?
27. How do we honor our parents?
28. What the significance of "That thy days may be long?"
29. Is it the same to kill as it is to murder?
30. When an officer of the land puts one to death "legally," is he guilty of murder?
31. In how many ways may one murder?
32. What is adultery?
33. What is fornication?
34. What is theft?
35. Can one steal and not be guilty under the law of our land?
36. Can I steal by contracting debts?
37. What is it to bear false witness?
38. In how many ways can one bear false witness?
39. Would Moses have borne false testimony by keeping silent?
40. What is it to covet?
41. Is it a sin to be wealthy?

THE TEN COMMANDMENTS

42. Name the points of difference between the covenant made at Mount Sinai and the New Covenant.
43. Quote a passage showing that the Ten Commandments are the Old Covenant.
44. What was on the tables of stone?
45. How many stones were there?
46. Why was the Old Covenant "taken out of the way?"
47. What was engraven in stones?
48. How long did the law last?
49. How was the law a schoolmaster?
50. Name the "positive" and the "moral" commandments.

PRAYER.

INTRODUCTION.

No subject has greater prominence in the Bible than prayer, and yet many Bible students are growing more indifferent to its blessings and privileges. The tendency of the times seems to be away from prayer. Perhaps no one can be entirely free from his environments; but to keep this prayerless spirit of the present age from overwhelming us, let us diligently read the ·Bible, and thus associate with God and Christ and the praying men of God—and pray. Prayer is the very breath of the Christian.

There are two essential elements in the Christian character—namely, a sense of obligation and a feeling of dependence. The neglect of either is hurtful. Obligation binds us to the discharge of certain duties; but a faithful discharge of duties has a tendency to create a feeling of self-satisfaction, and to eliminate the feeling of dependence. On the other hand, the feeling of dependence has a tendency to destroy the sense of obligation. A child that is petted and waited on by all the other members of the family soon reaches the point where it does not feel under any obligation to the rest of the family. There have been Christians, real and professed, who spent so much time in prayer, praise, and holy meditation that they lost sight of the practical duties of life. They spent their time gazing into heaven, and had no time to look about them on the fields white unto harvest. The well-rounded, forceful Christian life is made up of a proper blending of a sense of obligation and a feeling of dependence.

SOME HURTFUL THEORIES.

Many theories, even amongst professed Christians, have contributed greatly to the present neglect of prayer. Rationalism has crept into the church, and the teaching of the Bible on prayer is either ignored or explained away. With some theorists the plain statements of the Bible cease to be convincing, but everything must be subjected to the test of human reason. Strange as it seems, some of the most dogmatic of this class of rationalists are to be found amongst those who claim to take the Bible as their only guide. Their theories on prayer are not found in the Bible. On the subject of prayer, they do not ask, What does the Bible say? but, Is it possible for God to answer prayer.

1. GOD IS UNCHANGEABLE. It is argued that since God is unchangeable our prayers can have no effect. Such a conclusion is not found in the Bible. No inspired writer ever so argued. There are numerous examples of answered prayers. It does not meet the issue to say that all these occurred in the days of miracles; for, if the unchangeableness of God prevents his answering prayer now, it would have prevented it then, for he was unchangeable then as now. He answered prayer then. That is certain. Being unchangeable, he will answer prayer now. Thus the argument on the unchangeableness of God, instead of militating against prayer, is positive proof that God will now answer prayer.

2. GOD IS OMNISCIENT. It is contended that God possesses infinite wisdom and knows what we need before we ask him; that his nature being perfect, and his purposes always good, he will withhold no good thing from his children; hence, there can be no reason for praying. This view is the ground for many neglected prayers. Is it not true that all the foregoing was as true in Bible times as now? Prayers were answered then! It is foolish to argue against a demonstration. Do

not allow your zeal for argumentative ability to discredit the Bible.

3. MIRACLES HAVE CEASED. It is instisted that God cannot answer prayer without violating the law of nature, and that would be a miracle. Suppose that be true; if God says he will answer, are we going to subscribe to a theory that will make him a liar? Many who advocate this theory cannot define a natural law nor tell what a miracle is. How can one know that God cannot answer prayer without working a miracle? Do you know everything? If not, why make a statement which implies universal knowledge? If there is in all the universe one thing you do not know, that one thing may be how God can answer a prayer and not work a miracle. Do not make a fool of yourself trying to be smart.

A friend asks a favor, and you grant it. Did you work a miracle? The birds and beasts hear the cry of their young and bring them food—do they work miracles? We use the laws of nature every day to answer the requests, or prayers, of our friends, and children. Cannot God do as much? Jesus said: "With God all things are possible." But the advocates of this God-dishonoring theory make it possible for man and beast to do what they claim it is impossible for God to do.

That God cannot answer prayer without working a miracle is a mere assumption supported by no Bible teaching. So far as we understand the laws of nature, it is as much a miracle for God to hear us pray as it is for him to answer a prayer.

4. REFLEX INFLUENCE. By some we are told that reflex influence is the only benefit we derive from prayer. This makes prayer a sort of spiritual gymnasium in which we take spiritual exercise—and spiritual exercise is good, we are told! It is true that the reflex influence of a sincere prayer is good; but if prayer is

only a form of spiritual exercise and reflex influence is the only good derived therefrom, then the heathen is as much benefited by prayer as the Christian. Under what conditions are the reflex influences good? Would there be a good reflex influence if you pray to a post or stone? Your own heart answers: "No, the reflex influence would be bad." Why? Because you know the tree or stone cannot hear or answer? Such prayer would be foolish mockery. But is it any less so to pray to God believing he cannot hear and answer? In the very nature of the case the reflex influence of prayer is good only when we sincerely pray to One whom we believe hears us and is willing and able to grant us the desires of our hearts.

GOD ANSWERS PRAYERS.

The foregoing theories are not supported by the Bible, and no advocate of such theories ever tries to prove them by the Scriptures. Such theorists depend on a process of reasoning, and not on what God says. Not one of them points to a passage of Scripture and says: "This teaches my doctrine." They forgot that every Bible doctrine must be settled by what that Book says, and not by our reason. We should use our reason to learn what God says, and not to set aside what he teaches. Leave that to infidels. The proof that God answers prayer is too abundant to include all in this lesson, but we will briefly call attention to

THE BIBLE TEACHING ON PRAYER.

Jesus taught his disciples to pray (Matt. 6:5-15), and said: "Thy Father who seeth in secret shall recompense thee." "The eyes of Jehovah are toward the righteous, and his ears are open unto their cry" (Ps. 34:15).

"Ask, and it shall be given you; seek, and ye shall find; knock, and it shall be opened unto you: for every one that asketh receiveth; and he that seeketh findeth; and to him that knocketh it shall be opened. Or what man is there of you, who, if his son shall ask him for a loaf, will give him a stone; or if he shall ask for a fish, will give him a serpent? If ye then, being evil, know how to give good gifts unto your children, how much more shall your Father who is in heaven give good things to them that ask him?" (Matt. 7:7-11).

"The supplication of a righteous man availeth much in its working" (James 5:16). As an encouragement to prayer, James immediately adds: "Elijah was a man of like passions with us, and he prayed fervently that it might not rain; and it rained not on the earth for three years and six months. And he prayed again; and the heaven gave rain, and the earth brought forth her fruit" (vs. 17, 18). This was a remarkable prayer and answer, and the answer seems to have come in a natural way. To the people it did not appear as a miracle. (See I Kings, chapters 17 and 18).

PRAYING FOR WISDOM. "But if any of you lacketh wisdom, let him ask of God, who giveth to all liberally and upbraideth not; and it shall be given him" (James 1:5). God giveth to all liberally. How can one doubt what God says, if he believes in God? God does not promise in this text to give you knowledge—knowledge is information stored up in the mind, and is acquired by study, experience, and observation. Wisdom is tact, or skill, in the use of knowledge or any means to accomplish an end. Christians need Bible knowledge, and they need wisdom, or tact, that they may be able to properly use that knowledge. It is our duty as well as privilege to pray for wisdom.

PRAYING FOR OTHERS.

Paul prayed that his Jewish brethren might be saved. (Rom. 10:1). Certainly he did not pray for them to be saved in disobedience; and it would have been unnecessary for him to pray for God to save them when they obeyed God, for God would have done that without Paul's praying for their salvation. In his great desire for the salvation of his brethren he prayed that conditions and circumstances might be such as to lead them to accept the Lord Jesus as their Savior. Paul did not theorize; he worked and prayed. In fact, the theories now hindering some do not seem to have entered into the thinking of the early Christians. Their prayers pretty well covered the grounds of all Christian activities and material needs. Study closely the things Paul prayed for as indicated in Col. 1:9-12: "For this cause we also, since the day we heard it, do not cease to pray and make request for you, that ye may be filled with the knowledge of his will and all spiritual wisdom and understanding, to walk worthily of the Lord unto all pleasing, bearing fruit in every good work, and increasing in the knowledge of God; strengthened with all power, according to the might of his glory, unto all patience and long suffering with joy; giving thanks unto the Father, who made us meet to be partakers of inheritance of the saints in light." "I exhort therefore, first of all, that supplications, prayers, intercessions, thanksgivings, be made for all men; for kings and all that are in high place; that we may lead a tranquil and quiet life in all godliness and gravity" (I Tim. 2:1, 2).

Recognizing God's willingness to bless and his knowledge of what is best for us, let the Christian earnestly pray for whatever he longs for. When you have prayed for all you think you need, remember that God is "able to do exceeding abundantly above all that we ask or think, according to the power that worketh in us" (Eph. 3:20). "Let us therefore draw near with boldness unto the throne of grace, that we may receive mercy, and may find grace to help us in time of need" (Heb. 4:16).

PRAY ALWAYS.

On one occasion Jesus spoke "a parable unto them to the end that men ought always to pray, and not to faint" (see Luke 18:1-8). This parable teaches us to be persistent, importunate, in prayer, and not to grow weary, though the answer is long deferred. The parable:

"There was in a city a judge, who feared not God, and regarded not man: and there was a widow in that city; and she came oft unto him, saying, Avenge me of mine adversary. And he would not for a while; but afterwards he said within himself, Though I fear not God, nor regard man; yet because this widow troubleth me, I will avenge her, lest she wear me out by her continual coming. And the Lord said, Hear what the unrighteous judge saith, And shall not God avenge his elect, that cry to him day and night, and yet he is longsuffering over them? I say unto you, that he will avenge them speedily. Nevertheless, when the Son of man cometh, shall he find faith on the earth?"

The closing sentence is significant. Here was a widow making her plea to a selfish judge who had no regard for God or man, yet she believed in the righteousness of her cause and her heart was set on obtaining a favorable hearing, and she would not give up. She finally prevailed. Jesus assures us that God will avenge us, though he is longsuffering over us, and adds: "Nevertheless, when the Son of man cometh, shall he find faith on the earth?" That is, will he find people who have as much faith in God as this widow had in that perverse judge?

ACCEPTABLE PRAYER.

"Saying our prayers" is not necessarily praying. Are your prayers mere forms of words, cold and lifeless? Those who confine themselves to a set form of words when they pray are in danger of losing the spirit of prayer, and become no more than formalists. Prayer does not consist in beautiful expressions, devoutly uttered. Neither does prayer consist of solemn looks, pious tones, and humble attitude of the body. One can draw nigh unto God with his mouth and honor him with his lips, while his heart is far from him. Acceptable prayer is the blending of certain essential elements. These elements are sometimes referred to as conditions of acceptable prayer; but they are rather component parts, the essential elements, of acceptable prayer. Here are some of the elements of prayer:

1. DESIRE (Rom. 10:1). Without desire prayer would be an empty mockery.

2. REVERENCE. People sometimes approach God as if they thought they were his equal. "After this manner therefore pray ye: Our Father who art in heaven, Hallowed be thy name" (Matt. 6:9). "For all these things hath my hand made, and so all these things came to be, saith Jehovah: but to this man will I look, even to him that is poor and of a contrite spirit, and that trembleth at my word" (Isa. 66:2).

3. IN THE NAME OF CHRIST. "And whatsoever ye shall ask in my name, that will I do, that the Father may be glorified in the Son. If ye shall ask anything in my name, that will I do" (John 14:13, 14). "In the name of Christ," as here used, does not mean "by the authority of Christ," but rather that we approach the Father in prayer through Christ as our High Priest. In olden times the priest officiated for the people, and through or by him the people made their sacrifices. Christ is our High Priest, and through him, or in his name, we approach God; "for through him we both have our access in one Spirit unto the Father" (Eph. 2: 18). We are to "offer up spiritual sacrifices, acceptable to God through Jesus Christ" (I Peter 2:5).

4. SINCERELY. There is a temptation to pray to the

people rather than to God. We dislike for people to criticise our prayers, adversely, and are inclinded to pray to gain their approval. Jesus warns us against praying to be seen of men (Matt. 6:5). Such prayers are not sincere You should not take advantage of an occasion, and, while pretending to pray to God, deliver a sermon or exhortation to the people present.

5. THE SPIRIT OF OBEDIENCE AND WITHOUT SIN IN THE HEART. Jesus taught his disciples to pray: "Thy will be done, as in heaven, so on earth" (Matt. 6:10). If you pray thus, you desire God's will to be done in your own heart and life. "And whatsoever we ask we receive of him, because we keep his commandments and do the things that are pleasing in his sight" (I John 3:22). "He that turneth away his ear from hearing the law, even his prayer is an abomination" (Prov. 28:9). "If I regard iniquity in my heart, the Lord will not hear" (Ps. 66:18).

6. FAITH, CONFIDENCE. Why should any one pray if he does not believe God will hear? "But let him ask in faith, nothing doubting: for he that doubteth is like the surge of the sea driven by the wind and tossed. For let not that man think that he shall receive anything of the Lord; a doubleminded man, unstable in all his ways" (James 1:6-8). If you doubt the efficacy of prayer, this is your picture.

7. SUBMISSION. "If we ask anything according to his will, he heareth us" (I John 5:14). We must realize that God knows what is best for us, and that, therefore, he may not be willing to give us what we want. Like the Savior, we should say: "Nevertheless, not as I will, but as thou wilt" (Matt. 26:39).

8. FORGIVING. SPIRIT. "And forgive us our debts, as we also have forgiven our debtors ..... But if we forgive not men their trespasses, neither will your Father forgive your trespasses" (Matt. 6:12-15).

9. HUMILITY. Learn a lesson from the publican, who prayed with downcast eyes: "God, be thou merciful to me a sinner" (see Luke 18:9-14).

10. UNSELFISHNESS. It is not wrong to pray for what we need, but it is wrong to pray for things to gratify our lusts and selfish ambitions. "Ye have not, because ye ask not. Ye ask, and receive not, because ye ask amiss, that ye may spend it in your pleasure" (James 4:2, 3).

11. CONFESSING SINS. "If we confess our sins, he is faithful and righteous to forgive us our sins and to cleanse us from all unrighteousness" (I John 1:9).

THE PRAYER OF AN ALIEN SINNER.

Whether God will hear the prayer of an alien sinner has been a subject of much controversy. Certainly God will not hear the prayers of those who rebel at his commands, whether they be in the church or out. "He that turneth away his ear from hearing the law, even his prayer is an abomination" (Prov. 28:8). This was evidently spoken of disobedient Hebrews, for it did not occur to them that God would hear the prayers of any one else. "We know that God heareth not sinners: but if any man be a worshiper of God, and do his will, him he heareth" (John 9:31). This was said by an uninspired man whose eyes the Lord had opened. The leaders of the Jews said Jesus was a sinner, and the once-blind man defended him. Both knew that Jesus was a Hebrew, in covenant relationship with God; neither thought of him as an alien. The prayer of an alien was not under discussion. It is wrong, therefore, to apply this text to aliens.

WHO IS A SINNER? If a sinner is a rebel against God, one who disregards the law of the Lord, and is in the active service of the devil, will God hear such in prayer even if they should pray? No.

WHO IS AN ALIEN? Aliens are those who are not in covenant relationship with the Lord, those who have not entered into the kingdom or become citizens of the kingdom (see Eph. 2:12-22).

That God hears the prayers of aliens under certain conditions is proved by the fact that he heard the prayers of Cornelius and Saul of Tarsus. Cornelius prayed regularly to God. He must have prayed often to God to lead him to fully know his duty, for he was directed by an angel sent from God to send for Peter, who would tell him what to do (see Acts 10). Saul prayed, and God approved his prayers (see Acts 9:1-19; 22:3-16).

PUBLIC OR CONGREGATIONAL PRAYER.

You may wish to pray alone to God touching any desire of your heart. Do so. You should pray in secret for things that concern your personal or private affairs. Secret prayers should be in secret places (Matt. 6:5-8).

There are numerous examples of public prayers. In congregational prayer one leads as spokesman for the entire congregation, and the congregation follows and says "Amen." The congregation must understand what the leader says, else how can they say "Amen" to his prayer? (see I Cor. 14:16). This makes it binding on the leader in prayer or in giving thanks—

1. To use language that all can understand.

2. To speak loud enough for the entire congregation to hear him distinctly.

Many who are called on to lead the congregation in prayer fail miserably to do their duty. Some use language that many cannot understand, and some have the lazy habit of mumbling their words so low that only those very near them understand what they say. If the audience does not hear and understand the leader, he is not leading them in prayer. He is praying a private prayer in a public place.

PRAYER

Do not attempt to teach the congregation while praying.

Do not pray all day.

If you are called on to express thanks at the Lord's table, do not engage in a long prayer. Express thanks and quit.

* * *

TOPICS FOR INVESTIGATION AND DISCUSSION.

1. The Prayer of Jabez (I Chron. 4:9, 10).
2. The Model Jesus Gave the Disciples (Matt. 6:9-15).
3. The Prayer of Jesus (John 17).
4. Secret, or Individual, Prayer (Matt. 6:5-8).
5. Public, or Congregational, Prayer.
6. The Prayer of Aliens.

* * *

QUESTIONS.

1. Do you think people pray less than formerly?
2. What two essential elements in the Christian character?
3. What is the effect of neglecting either?
4. What is rationalism?
5. What is the theory of the unchangeableness of God?
6. What is the fallacy in this theory?
7. What the theory on the wisdom of God and his goodness?
8. Wherein does this theory break down?
9. What the theory about miracles in connection with prayer?
10. What is the law of nature?
11. What is a miracle?
12. Do we or the birds and beasts work miracles to answer the call of dependent ones?
13. Are we to make God more helpless than we are?
14. How do we hear?
15. How does God hear?
16. Is it a miracle for God to hear?
17. Can any one know that God cannot answer without working a miracle?

18. What the theory about the reflex influence of prayer?
19. What do you think of this theory, and why?
20. If God does not answer prayer, why may we not as well pray to an idol?
21. Under what condition would the reflex influence of prayer be good?
22. Is human wisdom or the Bible our guide?
23. By what authority do we determine that God answers prayer?
24. Do you know a passage of Scripture which to you means that God cannot or does not answer prayer?
25. What does Jesus say about God answering prayer?
26. What lesson does he give about our earthly father and our Heavenly Father?
27. What is true of the supplication of a righteous man?
28. What does James say about Elijah?
29. Tell about Elijah's prayer.
30. What should the man do who lacks wisdom?
31. What is the difference between knowledge and wisdom?
32. To whom does God give liberally?
33. What was Paul's prayer for his brethren?
34. What the difference between a desire and a prayer?
35. How could Paul's prayer for the brethren be answered?
36. Did early Christians advance theories against prayers?
37. For whom did Paul pray, as indicated in Col. 1:9-12?
38. What does Paul say in Eph. 3:26?
39. Why did Jesus speak the parable in Luke 18:1-8?
40. What is the character of that judge?
41. What is said about the widow?
42. Have you as much faith in your prayers to God as she had in her prayers to that perverse judge?
43. Are all prayers acceptable to God?
44. Discuss the first element of acceptable prayer named in this lesson.
45. What is "saying prayers?"
46. Discuss "Reverence."
47. Discuss "In the Name of Christ," and give scriputres touching same.
48. What is it to be sincere in prayer?
49. What does the Savior say about praying to be seen of men?
50. Should we pray sermons?
51. Quote I John 3:22.

PRAYER

52. What does David say in Ps. 66:18?
53. What does James say about the doubting man?
54. What is said about asking according to the will of God?
55. Repeat the prayer of Jesus in the garden (Matt. 26:32).
56. Tell about the prayer of the publican.
57. Who were the publicans?
58. What about forgiveness in prayer?
59. Why does James say we receive not? (James 4:2, 3).
60. Can you name other necessary elements, or condition, of prayer?
61. What is said about the prayers of sinners?
62. Who is a sinner?
63. What is meant by an alien sinner?
64. Did God ever hear the prayers of aliens?
65. For what were Saul and Cornelius praying?
66. After they were told what to do, would God have heard had they refused to obey?
67. What does Jesus teach concerning secret prayers (Matt. 6:5-8).
68. Give a scriptural example of public prayer.
69. When one leads in prayer, what should the congregation do?
70. What is the duty of one who leads in prayer?
71. Are the prayers recorded in the Bible as long as those you usually hear?
72. Do you pray regularly?
73. Should you pray or express thanks at the Lord's table?

THE FIRST CHAPTER OF ACTS.

TITLE OF THE BOOK. In the King James Version this book is called "The Acts of the Apostles." But this title is not entirely correct, for the book contains only some of the acts of some of the apostles. By some it is called "Acts of Apostles," but some of the deeds recorded were done by other than apostles. In the American Standard Version the title is simply "The Acts." It has also been called the "Book of Conversions." It is that, but more. It is really a brief history of the early church, the only absolutely reliable church history ever written.

Let the student seriously reflect over the fact that this is the only book of the Bible giving a record of the conversions under the Great Commission.

ITS AUTHOR. It is not stated in so many words who its author is; but Acts 1:1, 2, together with Luke 1:1-4, identifies the author of "The Acts" with the author of "The Gospel According to Luke." Read Luke 1:1-4, and then these verses in Acts 1: "The former treatise I made, O Theophilus, concerning all that Jesus began both to do and to teach, until the day in which he was received up, after that he had given commandment through the Holy Spirit unto the apostles whom he had chosen."

A CONTINUATION OF THE FORMER HISTORY. The foregoing verses show clearly that "The Acts" is a continuation of the former treatise, which closed with the returning of the disciples to Jerusalem after the ascension of Jesus. In Acts, Luke gives a fuller account of the incidents connected with the ascension.

"The commandment" mentioned in Acts 1:2 is evidently the Great Commission (Matt. 28:18-20; Mark 16:15, 16; Luke 24:46, 47). This commission is the key to "The Acts." The acts and preaching of the apostles is the best exposition of the meaning of the Great Commission.

"HIS PASSION." "To whom he showed himself alive after his passion by many proofs, appearing unto them by the space of forty days" (v. 3). Only here do we learn how long Jesus remained with his apostles after his resurrection. "His passion"—His suffering, crucifixion.

HIS IDENTITY. When Jesus was crucified his disciples gave up hope, and it took strong proof to reassure them. But during these forty days the apostles were with him in such intimate association that they could not have been mistaken in his identity. In addition to his apostles and others to whom he appeared frequently during the forty days, he was seen by more than five hundred brethren at one time (I Cor. 15:6).

SPEAKING THE THINGS CONCERNING THE KINGDOM OF GOD. He was soon to ascend to the Father and be crowned King, and the apostles as his ambassadors were to proclaim that fact and make known his laws. It was needful, therefore, that they have the fullest possible instructions. In the Great Commission we have summed up the fundamentals of his reign. For a fuller discussion of the Commission, the student is referred to "Sound Doctrine," Vol. I.

WAITING IN JERUSALEM. "Being assembled together with them, he charged them not to depart from Jerusalem, but to wait for the promise of the Father, which, said he, ye heard from me" (v. 4). Compare with Luke 24:36-49. "The promise of the Father" is the promise of the giving of the Holy Spirit, so often mentioned by the Savior, and dwelt on so much the night of his betrayal (see John 7:37-39; 14:16, 26; 15:25; 16:7-15). The matters which they were to teach were so important, and human nature so likely to fail, that Jesus specially charged them to wait in Jerusalem till the promised Spirit came, adding: "Ye shall be baptized in the Holy Spirit not many days hence." The baptism in the Holy Spirit was necessary to equip them as ambassadors of Christ and as revelators and executors of his will.

FALSE IDEAS OF THE KINGDOM. With all that Christ had taught the apostles concerning the kingdom, they did not comprehend his mission nor the nature of his kingdom. Their minds were so filled with the vision of the temporal kingdom restored, with Christ as a universal sovereign on the throne of David in Jerusalem, the whole world paying tribute, that they had utterly failed to see in him a universal sovereign, crowned King in heaven and ruling over a glorious spiritual kingdom. Even the hope of an earthly kingdom faded from their minds when Jesus died, but had been revived by his resurrection; hence, in his last interview with them, they said: "Lord, dost thou at this time restore the kingdom to Israel?" This question shows, at least, two things: (1) that the apostles still looked for their old kingdom to be restored; (2) that the kingdom of Christ had not at that time been established; for had it been established, his chief executors could not have been ignorant of its existence. Had such been possible, Jesus most certainly would have disabused their minds of such dense ignorance; but, instead, he declared: "It is not for you to know times or seasons, which the Father has set within his own authority." That is, God alone knows the times or seasons of the fulfillment of his promises or prophecies. It is not for man to be meddling into such matters. This rebuke of the Lord should be heeded by all prophetic speculators. "The secret things belong unto Jehovah our God; but the things which are revealed belong unto us and to our children forever, that we may do all the words of this law" (Deut. 29:29).

POWER PROMISED. "But ye shall receive power, when the Holy Spirit is come upon you." Only this miraculous endowment of the Holy Spirit would enable them to know any of the secret things of Jehovah. Such power had been repeatedly promised (Matt. 3:11; 10:19, 20; Mark 1:8; John 14:26; 16:7-13; Luke 24:49). When this power comes, "ye shall be my witnesses both in Jerusalem, and in all Judea and Samaria, and unto the uttermost part of the earth" (v. 8). For a discussion of the qualification of Christ's witnesses, the reader is referred to the lesson on "The Apostles" in "Sound Doctrine," Vol. I.

JERUSALEM. No one knows when Jerusalem was founded. It was called "Salem" in the days of Abraham (Gen. 14:8). It became the capital city of the Jews in the days of David. Here Solomon's temple was builded. It thus became the center of Jewish education, government, and religion. From this city the prophets, looking forward to newer and better things, said the law should go forth from Jerusalem (Isa. 2:1-4: Mic. 4:1-3). And here the apostles, at the command of Jesus, were to begin preaching in his name. They were to begin preaching Christ in the city of his greatest humiliation and amongst his bitterest enemies. Had they gone to some place remote from Jerusalem to begin their labors, the enemies could have exultantly said: "You could not have made any converts here, where every one knows the facts, so you went to the people ignorant of the facts to make your converts." But they were to begin amongst the very ones best prepared to disprove their claims and most interested in so doing. The benevolence and graciousness of his reign is also seen in that he offers pardon first to his murderers.

HIS ASCENSION. His last words having been spoken, "as they were looking, he was taken up; and a cloud received him out of their sight." From Luke's former account of the ascension, to which this is added as a supplement, we learn that Jesus with uplifted hands was in the act of blessing them when he ascended (Luke 24: 50, 51).

Two Men Stood by Them. It was but natural for the awe-stricken apostles to stand gazing in wonder and astonishment, even after the cloud had received him out of their sight. "Two men stood by them in white apparel." Evidently these were angels in the form of men, as this was a common form of expression (Matt. 28: 3-5; Luke 24: 24).

"Why Stand Ye Looking into Heaven?" This seems to have been a rebuke, and was doubtless intended to call their attention to present duties. It is necessary for us to look around us and see the needs before us, instead of putting in our time gazing into heaven, or into the future. Some present-day theorists need this rebuke.

Jesus Is Coming Again. These men or angels informed the apostles that Jesus, who had just departed from them into heaven, would "so come in like manner" as they had seen him go into heaven. This must refer to his final coming, at which time he will come personally, openly, visibly (Rev. 1: 7). At his coming the saints will meet him in the air (I Thess. 4: 14-17).

FROM THE ASCENSION TO PENTECOST.

"Then returned they unto Jerusalem from the mount which is called Olivet, which is nigh unto Jerusalem, a Sabbath day's journey off" (v. 12). A Sabbath day's journey is said to be seven-eights of a mile. On their return to Jerusalem they went into an upper chamber, their abiding place (v. 13). This was, perhaps, the upper room in which the Lord's Supper was instituted (Matt. 26: 26-28). Certainly it must have been in the house of one friendly to Christ, who, for this reason, turned this room over to the apostles as their abiding place during these days of waiting.

"These continued steadfastly in prayer with the women, and Mary the mother of Jesus, and with his brethren" (v. 14). Their manner of spending these days was such as might have been expected. It is not necessary to suppose that they spent the entire time in the upper chamber. Indeed, in his former treatise Luke specifically states that "they were continually in the temple, blessing God" (Luke 24:53). Here doubtless they met for prayers with the others mentioned. The way in which Luke mentions the women shows that he expected Theophilus to know to whom he made reference. Evidently he referred to the women mentioned in Luke 23:49, who had come with Jesus out of Galilee. This is the last time Mary the mother of Jesus is mentioned in the New Testament. His brethren, who did not formerly believe in him (John 7:1-5), are now amongst his devoted followers. These were brethren in the flesh, and their names are mentioned in Matt. 13:55; 27:56.

One of these meetings, at which about one hundred and twenty were present, is prominently mentioned because of a speech made by Peter and because at that time the Lord pointed out Matthias as the one to take the place of Judas in the apostleship.

JUDAS. In connection with the betrayal of Jesus by Judas, a question is frequently raised that involves the free moral agency and personal responsibility of Judas. If the betrayal of Jesus was a fulfillment of a prophecy, and if Jesus knew that Judas would betray him, how, then, we are asked, could Judas avoid it? Such questions show a desire to pry into things not revealed. Every man is conscious of the fact that he is a free moral agent. If he *is* not, then he should neither be blamed nor rewarded for anything he does; neither should he have any regrets for any act of his own, no matter how base. Why, then should Judas have been filled with such bitter remorse that he went and hanged himself? Or why should Jesus have denounced him as having a devil? And why should Peter say that by transgression he fell? If God were forcing him to do what he did, if he was only carrying out God's will in his own case, then what did he transgress? If he were not a free moral agent in betraying Christ, then he was not in his transgression or fall. But the whole trouble in the matter of the free moral agency of Judas grows out of the idea entertained by some that because Christ knew beforehand what Judas would do, Judas had no choice in the matter. It is argued that foreknowledge amounts to predestination, that God cannot foreknow a thing without predetermining it. That opens a vast field which we cannot enter, but which will be discussed in a later volume of this series of lessons. But this may be said now: Man cannot comprehend God, and cannot, therefore, know what is possible with God. To say that a certain thing is impossible with God is to limit the Infinite Being. Reverence should prevent a man from being dogmatic on such matters.

WAS JUDAS A DEVIL FROM THE BEGINNING?

Some good people hold the view that Judas was a devil from the beginning—i. e., that he was wicked all his life.

Of him we know nothing till he is mentioned as one of the twelve apostles (Matt. 10:4). He was one of the number Jesus sent forth to preach; he with the other apostles was given power to cast out devils (Mark 3:13-19), and Satan could not cast out Satan (Mark 3:22-27). Not only was he an apostle sent to preach and cast out devils, but he was called a friend of Jesus (Ps. 41:9).

Satan entered him at the close of the supper (John 13: 27)

We should remember, though, in the study that Jesus said of Judas: "Did I not choose you the twelve, and one of you is a devil?" (John 6:69). And again "While I was with them I kept them in thy name which thou hast given me: and I guarded them, and not one of them perished, but the son of perdition; that the scripture might be fulfilled" (John 17:12). In this Jesus speaks of Judas as having "perished." Certainly he had not at that time destroyed himself, and reference cannot be made to his self-destruction—his act of suicide; but he had turned from Christ, he had covenanted for the betrayal of Christ, Satan had entered him and he was being guided at that time by Satan, and as a disciple of Jesus he had certainly "perished." He could not have "perished" as a disciple had he not formerly been a disciple.

PETER'S SPEECH (Vs. 15-22).

Peter's speech was short and to the point. Observe that there are two parenthetical expressions inclosed in the speech. It is easily seen that they are Luke's words, thrown in for the purpose of explanation. Immediately after the word "said," in verse 15, Luke parenthetically tells the number present. Verses 18 and 19 are evidently Luke's words.

"The scripture..... which the Holy Spirit spake before by the mouth of David." This is a significant expression. The Holy Spirit spoke, but how? "By the mouth of David." Some seem to think that the Holy Spirit in some mystical way spoke to the inspired men, and then he spoke to the people. Not so; the Holy Spirit spoke to the people "by the mouth of David" and other inspired men. This is the Holy Spirit's method of talking to the people. Through the record left by these inspired men the Holy Spirit still speaks to men. Paul says: "Wherefore, even as the Holy Spirit saith, To-day if ye shall hear his voice, harden not your hearts" (Heb. 3:7-10). Here Paul quotes the scripture, and tells us it is what the Holy Spirit says. The Holy Spirit is speaking to you when you are reading the Bible. "He that hath an ear, let him hear what the Spirit saith to the churches" (Rev. 2:7).

In verses 18, 19 Luke explains some things about Judas. "This man obtained a field with the reward of his iniquity." Judas bargained with the chief priests to deliver Jesus into their hands for thirty pieces of silver (Matt. 26:14-16). Later, when Judas saw that Jesus was condemned, he was filled with remorse, and brought the money back to the chief priests. They took it and bought a piece of ground with it (Matt. 27:3-8). Inasmuch as this field was bought with Judas' money, it could truly be said that he obtained the field. It literally became a part of his estate, and could have been lawfully claimed by his heirs.

HOW JUDAS COMMITTED SUICIDE.

"Falling headlong, he burst asunder in the midst, and all his bowels gushed out" (v. 18). It is also said that Judas hanged himself (Matt. 27:5). Is there a lack of harmony between Luke and Matthew? We see none. After Judas hanged himself, Luke says he fell. If he remained hanging for several days, as most likely he did, or if the rope broke and he fell a great distance immediately after he hanged himself, it is but natural that the results should have been as Luke says they were.

From this circumstance Luke says the field was called the "field of blood." Some think this contradicts Matt. 27:6, 7, where it is called the "field of blood" because it was bought with the price of blood. There is no contradiction—both facts make it appropriate to speak of it as the "field of blood."

DAVID QUOTED.

In verse 20 Peter quotes from the Psalms (69:23; 109:8). In both Psalms it appears that David was speaking of the wicked in general, but what was true of the wicked in general would certainly be true of so base a character as Judas.

SUCCESSOR OF JUDAS.

"Of the men therefore that have companied with us all the time..... must one becomes a witness with us of his resurrection" (vs. 21, 22). Here Peter makes known the necessary qualifications for a successor of an apostle. Only two men could be found then possessing the requisite qualifications—namely, Joseph and Matthias. None can be found now, for none now living were with Jesus from the baptism of John till the ascension of the Master.

AN OBJECTION CONSIDERED.

It is said by some that the apostles had no right to act in this matter, for the Savior had specially charged them to wait the coming of the Holy Spirit. The objection is not well founded, and the proof given to support the objection is not to the point. Certainly they were not to begin preaching till they were inspired by the Spirit, but does it follow that they were to do nothing? Luke says: "They were continually in the temple, blessing God" (Luke 24:33), and "these all with one accord continued steadfastly in prayer" (Acts 1:14). Did they have a right to thus serve and worship God? Besides if Jesus during the forty days had given them no instructions concerning the matter, how did such a matter occur to them? And had the idea occurred to one of them, some of the company most certainly would have objected to the procedure had there been no authority for it. Finally, had they been making the selection, they would have needed the illumination of the Holy Spirit to make the right selection. They found two in their company possessing the necessary qualifications, and let the Lord show which one he had chosen. (The reader is referred to "Sound Doctrine," Vol. I., pages 86, 87, for a further discussion of this question.)

* * *

TOPICS FOR INVESTIGATION AND DISCUSSION.

Judas.
Jerusalem in Old and New Testaments.
Second Coming of Jesus.
This Life the Time for Preparation to Meet God.
Prominent People Who Became Christians in Days of Apostles.

* * *

QUESTIONS.

1. What is meant by King James Version?
2. By what name is the fifth book of the New Testament called?
3. What history found in this book?
4. Who is the author of The Acts?
5. Who was Theophilus?
6. What relation does the Great Commission bear to The Acts?
7. How long was Jesus with the apostles after his resurrection?
8. What is means by his "passion?"
9. Could the apostles have been mistaken in the identity of Jesus?
10. To how many did he appear?
11. To whom did he appear the last time?
12. Of what did Jesus talk after his resurrection?
13. What promise did he bid them wait for in Jerusalem?

THE FIRST CHAPTER OF ACTS

14. For what kind of a kingdom were the disciples looking?
15. What question did they direct to Christ?
16. What two things did their question reveal?
17. Repeat the reply Christ made to their question.
18. What, if any, was the rebuke in the question?
19. What do you think about speculators?
20. Why the baptism in the Holy Spirit?
21. What was necessary of being a witness for Christ?
22. When was Jerusalem founded?
23. By what names has it been called?
24. Where was the temple of Solomon builded?
25. When and by whom was it destroyed?
26. When and by whom was it rebuilded?
27. When destroyed the last time? By whom?
28. Quote the prophecy showing the law was to go forth from Jerusalem.
29. Why begin in Jerusalem
30. From what point did Jesus ascend?
31. What was he doing as he began to ascend?
32. What did the disciples do?
33. Who stood by them?
34. Was there a rebuke in what they said?
35. How will Jesus come again?
36. Who will see him when he comes?
37. Where will the saints meet him?
38. What distance was a Sabbath days' journey?
39. Why did they return to Jerusalem?
40. How did they spend their time?
41. Who is mentioned as being with them?
42. Give the names of the brothers of Jesus.
43. How many were present when Matthias was named an apostle?
44. Was Judas a free moral agent?
45. Was Judas responsible?
46. Does foreknowledge equal predetermination?
47. Was Judas a devil from the beginning?
48. Was Judas an apostle?
49. Was he given power to cast out devils?
50. Was he a friend of Jesus?
51. When did Satan enter Judas?
52. Did Judas partake of the Lord's Supper?
53. What is meant when Jesus said Judas "perished?"

54. Could he "perish" as a disciple if he had not been a disciple?
55. How does the Holy Spirit speak?
56. What did Judas do with the money he received for betrayal of Jesus?
57. Reconcile the statements about the death of Judas.
58. What quotation does Peter make from David?
59. Who succeeded Judas?
60. Who selected Matthias?
61. Who else possessed the qualifications to be a witness—apostle?

THE JERUSALEM CHURCH.

The Jerusalem church has been called the "mother church," because it was the first church of God in the Christian dispensation, and from it all others directly or indirectly sprang. The second chapter of Acts gives a record of the events connected with the establishment of this church, together with some statements concerning its early history. The church prospered for a time, but was finally scattered by persecution. In the first seven chapters of Acts you will find a record of the prosperity of this church. In the first verses of the eighth chapter you will find the record of the scattering of this church by persecution.

THE FIRST CHURCH OF GOD.

Some contend that the church was established before the First Pentecost after the resurrection of Christ, but no one can point out a local congregation prior to this date. It is true that some of the material of this congregation was prepared and collected in Jerusalem before Pentecost, just as one collects material for a house to be built, but it was not organized so as to perform its functions till that day.

Careful and unbiased scholars and historians have always recognized the First Pentecost after the resurrection of Christ as the beginning of the first church of God.

HISTORIANS.

The great Baptist, Dr. J. B. Jeter, says: "The first church was formed in Jerusalem, and soon became the mother of other churches in various countries."—Baptist Principles Reset, p. 21.

Again, Dr. Jeter says: "It has already been shown

that the first church was organized in the city of Jerusalem, after the ascension of Jesus, and was composed entirely of believers."—Ibid., p. 27.

Referring to the events of Pentecost: "And here we contemplate the beginning of the establishment of Christ's kingdom in the world; or, which is the same thing, **the erection of the first Christian church.**"—Jones' Church History.

"The church at Jerusalem was the first Christian church established by the ministry of the apostles."—Ibid., p. 70.

"The first of all the Christian churches founded by the apostles was that of Jerusalem."—Mosheim's Eccl. Hist. (Murdock's Translation), Vol. I., p. 46.

"This Christian assembly, as it was the first, so it is the mother church in the Christian dispensation."—Orchard's History of Baptist, p. 7).

ITS ACTIVITIES.

A brief summary of the activities of this first church is given in Acts 2:42: "And they continued steadfastly in the apostles' teaching and fellowship, in the breaking of bread and the prayers."

TEACHING. The new converts would, of course, know little or nothing of their Christian duties and of the practical affairs of the church, nor of the fundamental doctrines of Christianity. And former disciples of Christ, many of whom were present, needed further enlightenment. Had they returned home immediately after being baptized, much of the labor of that memorable day would have been lost, for in their ignorance they could not have lived the Christian life. Properly taught, they would be a power for good wherever they went. Hence, that they might be efficient servants of Jehovah in their various homes, the apostles carried them through a period of intensive training and teaching. All recognized the apostles as Christ's chosen teachers, and so continued in "the apostles' teaching." Continuing in the apostles' teaching cannot mean that they continued to do what the apostles taught, for doing what they taught is mentioned in a separate item—viz., "Fellowship, in the breaking of bread and the prayers." It can mean no more than that they continued under the instruction of the apostles.

The apostles discharged the duty which Jesus enjoined on them in the Great Commission—to teach those baptized (Matt. 28:19, 20). It was just as much the duty of those baptized to be taught as it was the duty of the apostles to teach them. It is as much our duty now to be taught as it was theirs. Few realize that God requires us to learn the Bible, and that it is a grievous sin not to study it. "Learn of me," said Jesus (Matt. 11:29). "Let the word of Christ dwell in you richly" (Col. 3:16).

FELLOWSHIP. Fellowship is joint participation. The Greek word, "koinoonia," is sometimes used for contributions made for the poor (Rom. 15:25; II Cor. 9:13). By their gifts they were having fellowship with the poor in their sufferings. But the word does not always have reference to contributions. We have such expressions as "the fellowship of his Son Jesus Christ" (I Cor. 1:9); "the fellowship ["communion"—A. S. V.] of the Holy Spirit" (II Cor. 13:14); "that ye also may have fellowship with us: yea, and our fellowship is with the Father, and his Son Jesus Christ" (I John 1:3). Fellowship is a joint participation in the sufferings, hardships, duties, and privileges belonging to the Christian life. It, therefore, sometimes means contributions.

BREAKING OF BREAD. This evidently refers to the Lord's Supper. For a discussion of this subject, see "Sound Doctrine," Vol. I., pages 168-183.

THE PRAYERS. Jesus prayed, the inspired men prayed, the Jerusalem church continued in prayer. Prayer is a vital part of the Christian's life. It is regretable that certain theories about natural law has so corrupted the minds of some that they see no special need for prayer. Let no human theory rob you of the blessing and privilege of prayer.

While all the items mentioned in Acts 2:42 should enter into the Lord's day worship, it is hurtful and sinful to try to bind them on a congregation in the order mentioned. To do so is to bind where God has not bound. Without going into detail here, we will say that the thoughtful reader can easily see reasons why prayers should precede the other items of worship.

UNITY OF THE JERUSALEM CHURCH.

Jesus prayed that his followers might be one (John 17:20, 21). This unity prayed for by the Master was manifested in the Jerusalem church, for Luke says they continued "steadfastly with one accord" (Acts 2:46). Again: "And the multitude of them that believed were of one heart and soul" (Acts 4:32). This can mean nothing more than that the most delightful harmony prevailed in that church. It is a condition toward which every church should strive (Eph. 4:3).

ATTITUDE OF THE PEOPLE.

"Having favor with all the people." That this church, so soon after the crucifixion of Christ and amongst those who crucified him, should gain such universal favor with the people is exceedingly remarkable. Such earnestness, zeal, and unselfishness on the part of the early Christians commended them to the people, and gave them great favor. It means something in the eyes of the people to be a member of the church. Not by seeking popularity, but by self-forgetfulness in their desire to serve, they gained that degree of popular esteem which no man can gain by mere seeking for it. Would you have your church to stand so well in your community? Then lead it into like service. We do not need a "Twentieth Century" church, but what we need is the church the Lord established—we need that church in the twentieth century. Is the church of which you are a member that church? The first century church will function and prosper in the twentieth century if given a chance.

LIBERALITY OF THE JERUSALEM CHURCH.

We speak of their liberality in the use of their means. This liberality is mentioned in Acts 2:44, 45; 4:32-36; 6:1-6. Theirs was a remarkable manifestation of liberality, and has been the cause for some speculation. Some think these early Christians were Communists—that is, that there was no individual ownership of property. The rather prominent preachers taught that this early church tried the community of goods as an experiment, and as a consequence were reduced to want, so that churches elsewhere had to send to their relief, and, finding it a failure, they went back to individual ownership. To say that these Spirit-guided apostles experimented in this matter, how may we know what is experiment and what is not? And to say that this course brought them to such destitution that other churches had to send relief to them shows dense ignorance of the facts of history that one is made to wonder; for those who were parties to this liberality were all scattered from Jerusalem, and years passed before any relief was sent to Jerusalem. Even then it was because of the general drought throughout that whole region.

That there was no community of goods is evident to one who carefully reads the record. "They sold their possessions and goods, and parted them to all, according as any man had need" (Acts 2:45). "As many as were possessors of lands or houses sold them, and brought the prices of the things that were sold" (Acts 4:34). They did not pool their interests—they sold them. Ready cash was needed. There was individual ownership, else individuals could not have sold anything. Barnabas, who had a field, sold it (Acts 4:36, 37). This was some time after the church began.

ANANIAS AND SAPPHIRA. When Ananias and Sapphira sold their land, and, while professing to bring all, they brought only a part of the price, Peter said: "While it remained, did it not remain thine own?" This indicates clearly that Peter recognized their right of ownership. "And after it was sold, was it not in thy power?" Peter virtually tells them that they did not have to sell their possessions—it was theirs—and that, having sold it, they were not compelled to bring the price. Their sin was in lying about bringing the whole amount when they did not.

THE OCCASION FOR SELLING THEIR PROPERTY. The facts are that many of these first converts had come from their homes in various parts of the world to attend the feast of Pentecost (Acts 2:5-11). Should they immediately return to their homes without being taught and well grounded in their new-found religion, they would fall away; at least, they certainly would not know how to defend themselves, or go on in their Christian life, and the means of planting the cause of Christ in their respective communities. Hence, instead of returning home at once, they continued under the instruction of the apostle. Being so far from home, with no means of a livelihood, if they would remain long enough to be properly taught, some one must meet the demands of the occasion. Those who lived there and who had possessions did not selfishly regard their possessions as their own so long as the Lord's cause needed it. Each one, because of the great urgency, regarded his own property as if it belonged to all, and, as the need arose, sold it, and distribution was made as the need arose.

Is there a lesson in this for us?

You should be willing to give all, if necessary, to save the cause of Christ from perishing in your community, even to your own life. How much, then, should a man give? Give all, if necessary.

How Much Am I Able to Give? A word of caution before passing from this subject. These early Christians did not give more than they were able, though they gave all. One is able to give all he has. Ananias and Sapphira claimed to give all; but they lied about it, and died. Many brethren say they are giving all they are able when they still have some left. Remember, man is able to give all he has. You may on any occasion give all you should be expected to give, or even more; but, when giving generously and liberally, do not mar the gift by saying you are giving all you are able. Remember Ananias and Sapphira—they died for lying.

THE FIRST DEACONS.

It should be remembered that every organization of a business or philanthropic nature must have some one to look after its financial affairs. In too many churches the business affairs are regarded as of minor importance and sadly neglected. In the Jerusalem church it seems that the apostles had in their hands the affairs of the congregation for a time; but this phase of the work became so great, and the demand for their time in other lines so urgent, that they determined to be relieved from the duties incident to the care of the finances and just distribution amongst the needy.

Many of the Jews in their dispersed condition learned to speak the Greek language, and some of them continued to speak the Hebrew tongue. Within the pale of the Jerusalem church there were these two classes—

those who spoke Hebrew and those who spoke Greek. Alike they contributed of their means into the church treasury, and distribution was made amongst the needy. Growing out of what some of them thought was partiality there "arose a murmuring of the Grecian Jews against the Hebrews."

When this condition arose, the apostles called the multitude of the disciples unto them, and said: "It is not fit that we should forsake the word of God, and serve tables. Look ye out, therefore, brethren, from among you seven men of good report, full of the Spirit and wisdom, whom we may appoint over this business." The congregation selected the men, and the names indicate that they were Greeks—that they were from amongst the very ones who had complained.

These were the first deacons—the first ones selected by the congregation to be their servants in this business capacity. A deacon is but a servant of the congregation.

INCOMPETENT MEN. In too many instances congregations give the business affairs of the church into the hands of men who are not capacitated for the work assigned them. Men who are business failures are often selected to be deacons in the church, and then the church bemoans the fact that they are financially unable to do constructive work or alleviate the suffering of the needy about them. In many instances the evangelist, a stranger in the community, selects the elders and deacons. In the Jerusalem church, though the apostles were present, they instructed the church to select the men to serve the church as deacons—to select the men to see after the business of the congregation. The church made the selection.

You would not select a man to take charge of your business if you knew the man to be a business failure.

Do you think it is wise for the church to select a man, be he ever so pious and devoted, who has failed in a business way all his life, to have charge of the business of the church? Piety and devotion are not the only essentials to the work of the deacon. Remember the deacons, the first deacons selected, were to have in their hands the administration of business affairs. They were wise men, surely they were wise men in the work for which they were selected. Jesus said: "The sons of this world are for their generation wiser than the sons of light" (Luke 16:8). How often is this true in the business affairs of the church? It should not be thought that the work of the deacons in the business affairs of the church is of no importance. (In a subsequent copy of this series we will discuss fully the officers of the church and their work).

DISCIPLINE.

The Jerusalem church was, we think, as near perfect as could be made out of the material of which it was formed—the members were human, as we are. So long as we live on earth we will be subjected to temptations and sin. Discipline is necessary, not only for our good, but for the good of society. In all organizations composed of human beings there must be some corrective measures, for there will ever be found those who have not a proper regard for the rights of others. When man becomes a positive detriment to society, or by corrective measures he cannot be brought to respect the rights of others, he must be removed from society.

Possibly there is no one thing which so impedes the progress of the church as the laxity of discipline in some sections and the flagrant disregard of the Master's teaching on discipline.

Ananias and Sapphira, members of the Jerusalem church, sold their property; more, they agreed between themselves to pretend to cast the entire amount into the Lord's treasury while keeping back a portion. They would parade and advertise their liberality while acting a lie. Liars are a detriment to society, the church, and the State. The greatest measure known on earth, the gospel of Jesus Christ, and the association of men and women who were devoted to the principles of Christianity had failed to keep these two members in the right way. They sinned—deliberately lied to God. For such characters to have remained in the fellowship of the congregation would have resulted in untold injury to the church, for in time their hypocrisy would have been apparent; and had it not been exposed at the time of the attempted deception, young members of the church might have questioned the ability of the Holy Spirit to search and to know human hearts, or they might have concluded that deception was licensed if it was connected with liberality.

THE PENALTY. You may think the infliction of the extreme penalty, death, was out of proportion as punishment to the crime. Jehovah is wiser than we. He knows best. We do not know what the results might have been had they not been removed.

Let us learn this lesson: God does not approve of liars in the church. The Jerusalem church furnishes the example of the removal of such members—we must not fellowship with them. The congregation which disregards the injunction to expunge from her fellowship those who do not live right will not prosper.

Some may fear that if discipline is rigidly enforced but few would become members of the church. You should have no fears. The Lord knows best. Immediately following the death of Ananias and Sapphira there was a wonderful increase in the membership of the Jerusalem church.

(In a subsequent volume we will discuss at length "Church Discipline.")

THE JERUSALEM CHURCH

TOPICS FOR INVESTIGATION AND DISCUSSION.
1. Needs of the Church.
2. Why and When Withdraw from Members?
3. Should the Church Engage in Business?
4. Why Was the Church Popular?
5. The Church a Blessing in the Community.

* * *

QUESTIONS.
1. When and by whom was Jerusalem founded?
2. When did it become the chief city of the Jews?
3. Tell of its location.
4. In what country is Jerusalem?
5. When was Jerusalem destroyed the last time?
6. For many years who had control of Jerusalem?
7. Why is the Jerusalem church called the "mother church?"
8. Was there a church in the Old Dispensation?
9. What is Pentecost? (see Deut. 16:9-12).
10. How often did it come?
11. Why were the apostles in Jerusalem on the first Pentecost after the resurrection of Christ?
12. Tell what occurs as related in Acts 2:1-4.
13. Did the multitude come together to hear preaching?
14. Must one always come to hear preaching to be benefited?
15. Give the concluding statement of Peter's sermon on Pentecost.
16. What effect did his sermon have on the people?
17. What answer did Peter give to their inquiry?
18. Who were baptized?
19. How many were baptized?
20. How many were added?
21. How were they added?
22. What do historians say about Jerusalem?
23. Of what class of people was this church composed?
24. Quote the Great Commission (Matt. 28:18-20).
25. Where were the apostles to begin their work under the Great Commission (Luke 24:46-49)?
26. Why would baptized people need preaching?
27. What did Jesus command the apostles to teach them?
28. What is meant by "fellowship?"

29. What is meant by "breaking of bread?"
30. What is prayer?
31. Name some theories that hinder prayer?
32. Tell why we should pray.
33. Can you instance some congregational prayers?
34. In our Lord's day worship is it essential that we follow the order in which these items are mentioned in Acts 2:42?
35. Give some reasons why prayer should come before some other items.
36. Repeat a passage of scripture teaching such.
37. What expression declares the unity of the church?
38. Was this a popular church?
39. What gave it favor with the people?
40. Should the church be popular today?
41. Tell of the liberality of the Jerusalem church.
42. Did they practice communism?
43. Were Ananias and Sapphira members of the church?
44. In what did they sin?
45. What the occasion for sale of property?
46. What the necessity for the prolonged stay of the members in Jerusalem?
47. How much are you able to give?
48. How much should one give?
49. Is it any one's business how much I give?
50. Who were the first deacons in the church?
51. How were they chosen?
52. Why were they chosen?
53. What kind of men should be selected for deacons?
54. What two classes of Jews were in the church at Jerusalem?
55. What the cause of the murmuring in the Jerusalem church?
56. What party murmured?
57. From what party were the deacons selected?
58. Why is discipline necessary?

CONVERSION OF THE SAMARITANS.

LESSON TEXT: Acts 8:1-25.
MEMORY VERSES: Rom. 1:16, 17.

THE CITY OF SAMARIA.

The city of Samaria was builded by Omri, the sixth king of Israel (I Kings 16:23, 24), and thereafter was the capital city of the kingdom of Israel, being later taken by Shalmaneser, king of Assyria (II Kings 18:9, 10). It is now a "squalid and fanatical Moslem village whose paths and fields are cluttered with a multitude of fallen columns."

THE SAMARITANS.

When the king of Assyria captured the kingdom of Israel, he carried the people out of the land of Samaria and repeopled the land with heathen peoples from Babylon, Cuthah, Avva, Hamath, and Sepharvaim (II Kings 17:22-24). At the request of the people the king sent a priest of Israel back to this land to teach the people the manner of the God of the land (II Kings 17:25-29). They gradually outgrew their idolarty and adopted the Pentateuch as their law. There was never much sympathy between them and the Jews. When they were refused the privilege of assisting in rebuilding the temple in Jerusalem, they became very angry. Their anger finally grew into bitter enmity, so that they refused the Jews passage through their land. This enmity had considerably subsided in the days of Jesus, as is shown by his reception at Sychar, a city of Samaria (John 4).

LEADING UP TO THE LESSON

After the gospel began to be preached in Jerusalem, the apostles for some time, perhaps two years, confined their labors to Jerusalem, preaching only to Jews. Vast multitudes became Christians. These multitudes were being trained for the great work of carrying the gospel to others. Finally the great persecution arose against the church on the occasion of the martyrdom of Stephen, and the entire church was scattered abroad, except the apostles (Acts 8:1).

THE SCATTERED CHURCH.

"They were all scattered abroad throughout the regions of Judea and Samaria, except the apostles." But this seemingly great calamity did not break their spirit nor cool their zeal. "They therefore that were scattered abroad went about preaching the word" (Acts 8:4). They went about evangelizing, for so the original word signifies. Perhaps only a small part of them delivered public addresses; certainly the women did not; yet they all, men and women, went about evangelizing. Evangelizing is preaching the gospel, whether to multitudes assembled or to individuals, whether at home or abroad. They went evangelizing—that is, they evangelized as they went. The very form of the expression shows that the going and the evangelizing were different acts.

PHILIP.

Amongst the very active ones driven out of Jerusalem by this persecution was Philip, one of the seven chosen to serve the church in Jerusalem (Acts 6:1-6). Later he was referred to as Philip the evangelist (Acts 21:8). When the church at Jerusalem was scattered his services as deacon, of course, ceased; and, by virtue of the fact that he then gave his time to preaching the word, he became Philip the evangelist. He was not "set apart" as a preacher by some ecclesiastical body. The apostles had been filing the church with the word, and any Christian who became as full of the word as was Philip would preach it. To the extent any one preaches the word, to that extent he is an evangelist, for an evangelist is one who preaches the word.

Of Philip's early life we know nothing. He is first mentioned in connection with the seven chosen to serve tables (Acts 6). The eighth chapter of Acts gives a record of some of his work as a preacher. We hear no more of him till mention is made of him in Acts 21:8. At this time his home was in Cesarea, and he was called Philip the evangelist.

PREACHING CHRIST.

"AND PHILIP WENT DOWN TO THE CITY OF SAMARIA" (Acts 8:5). This is not Philip the apostle, for the apostles remained at Jerusalem (Acts 8:1), but it is Philip the deacon, who with others was chosen to serve tables (Acts 6).

"AND PROCLAIMED UNTO THEM THE CHRIST" (Acts 8:5). The Christ was the burden of the preaching of God's inspired preachers. "For I determined not to know anything among you, save Jesus Christ, and him crucified," said Paul (I Cor. 2:2). But what is it to preach Christ? Evidently to preach the gospel and to preach Christ is the same, for Philip was carrying out the Great Commission to preach the gospel. Though Paul determined to know nothing among the Corinthians save Jesus Christ and him crucified, he declared to them that he preached the gospel to them (I Cor. 15:1). Preaching the gospel, preaching Christ, and preaching the word are all the same, for in describing the planting of the church in Corinth, where Paul declares he preached the gospel (I Cor. 15:1), where he affirms that he preached Christ (I Cor. 2:2), Luke declares that

Paul dwelt in Corinth a year and a half, "teaching the word of God among them" (Acts 18:11). In our lesson it is declared that those who "were scattered abroad went about preaching the word," and it is declared that Philip was one of those who went about preaching the word, and that he preached Christ to the people of Samaria. To preach Christ, therefore, is to preach his word, the gospel. "For Moses from generations of old hath in every city them that preach him, being read in the synagogues every Sabbath" (Acts 15:21). Hence, reading and teaching the law of Moses was preaching Moses. The same is true of preaching Christ.

PREACH CHRIST—LET OTHER FOLKS ALONE. Christ is the Son of God, the Savior of man, prophet, priest, and king. These titles grow out of his relationship to God and man, and to preach him fully all the relationships indicated by the various names applied to him must be shown. In preaching him fully no man can "just preach Christ and let other folks alone." To preach him as the Son of God one must antagonize infidels. If he is preached as the Savior, the question naturally presents itself: "Will he save every one?" If you properly answer this question you will antagonize the Universalist—you can't preach Christ and let him alone. If he will not save every one, then whom will he save? Will he save only the "elect," as taught by the Calvinist? The gospel preacher, or teacher, cannot answer this question and let other folks alone. If the Calvinist doctrine of "election" is not true, then whom will be saved? Will Christ save people without conditions to be performed by them? If not, then what are the conditions of salvation? In answering this question fully, scripturally, the teacher, or preacher, will antagonize every denominationalist in the land. It is certain Philip told the Samaritans what to do to be saved.

CHRIST AS GOD'S PROPHET, God's message bearer,

CONVERSION OF THE SAMARITANS

God's teacher to man (Heb. 1:1, 2). A prophet is one who speaks for another, one who delivers the message of another. Hence, God's prophet is God's spokesman. The essential idea is that a prophet speaks for God. As God's prophet to man, what did Jesus teach? Here again every faithful teacher must come in conflict with every theory out of harmony with the teaching of Christ.

CHRIST THE HIGH PRIEST. Christ is our High Priest. There is a difference between the significance of the words "prophet" and "priest." The prophet is God's representative to man, the priest is man's representative to God. We are all priests (Rev. 1:6), but Christ is our High Priest—through him we approach God. To properly develop and present the New Testament idea of the priesthood is to antagonize every priestly order in the ecclesiasticisms of today.

CHRIST AS KING. As such he has laws—what are they? His kingdom has subjects—who are they? How may one enter the kingdom? In preaching Christ Philip gave answer to all these questions, for the record says: "When they believed Philip preaching good tidings concerning the kingdom of God and the name of Jesus Christ" (Acts 8:12). In preaching Christ as Philip did, and there is no other way to preach him, the gospel preacher cannot "let other people alone." Can you name one thing you can preach, or teach, fully and not conflict with some denominational doctrine? Away with the compromising spirit of the age, and pray: "Grant unto thy servant to speak thy word with all boldness" (Acts 4:29).

THE RESULTS OF PHILIP'S PREACHING.

"AND THE MULTITUDES GAVE HEED WITH ONE ACCORD UNTO THE THINGS THAT WERE SPOKEN BY PHILIP" (v. 6). Not ofter ha such favorable results followed any man's preaching The signs that Philip did, or the miracles that were wrought through him, showed the people that God was with him. These signs confirmed his preaching. The miracles did not convert them, but attracted the attention of the people and proved to them that Philip was a teacher from God. The purpose of miracles in connection with a preacher's work was to confirm the word (Mark 16:20; Heb. 2:2-4).

When Philip reached the city of Samaria, he found the people under the spell of one Simon, a magician, who had completely captivated them, and they regarded him as a great man. The works of Simon were then, as such works are now, astonishing to the people, and to the masses they were inexplicable; but, after all, such works are mere tricks, and the workers of them seek self-aggrandizement, or to bewilder the people. Philip came in direct conflict with the works of this magician, this wonder worker in Samaria. No sooner were the miracles he performed compared with the works of Simon than the people saw that Simon was a mere trickster; whereas Philip brought them blessings, for the people were healed of diseases and the lame made whole. The people were convinced that Philip was sent from God.

"AND THERE WAS MUCH JOY IN THAT CITY." Certainly there was great joy, for unclean spirits were cast out of many and many having fleshly infirmities were healed. And besides this, a new, glorious light had come to them.

WHAT THE PEOPLE DID.

"But when they believed Philip preaching good tidings concerning the kingdom of God and the name of Jesus Christ, they were baptized, both men and women." Luke's record of this conversion is brief, his language simple and plain. Philip preached, the people believed, and were baptized. The narrative is in perfect

CONVERSION OF THE SAMARITANS

harmony with the Great Commission, both as to the conditions and the simplicity of the language. "Go ye into all the world, and preach the gospel to the whole creation. He that believeth and is baptized shall be saved; but he that disbelieveth shall be condemned" (Mark 16:15, 16). The preaching was done first, accompanied by miracles to prove the trustworthiness of the message, and the people believed. "So belief cometh of hearing, and hearing by the word of Christ" (Rom. 10:17). And Peter says: "Brethren, ye know that a good while ago God made choice among you, that by my mouth the Gentiles should hear the word of the gospel, and believe" (Acts 15:17).

BELIEVED AND WERE BAPTIZED. "They were baptized, both men and women." From this it is seen that in preaching Christ unto men Philip taught them to be baptized, for there was no other way for them to learn this duty. "He that believeth and is baptized shall be saved," said the Lord. These people believed and were baptized; hence, they were saved. It is expressly stated that they believed before they were baptized. It must follow, then, that there was not an infant in the number baptized. More, there was not a church there to vote on them to determine whether the minister should baptize them!

SIMON.

Even Simon, who had been practicing his magic and bewitching the people, saw the superiority of the miracles wrought through Philip over his tricks of sorcery. To give up his pretentions to greatness and to come down from the pedestal on which the admiring public had placed him and sit at the feet of Philip like the humblest and most ignorant, required a greater effort and more self-abasement than most pretentious people are willing to make. But he did. "And Simeon also himself believed: and being baptized," in this new-found joy, he "continued with Philip."

WAS SIMON SAVED? This question would never have been raised had it not been that after his baptism he fell into grievous sin. More, were it not for the doctrine that it is impossible for a child of God to fall from grace, so far fall as to be lost, as taught by Baptists and Presbyterians, the question as to the salvation of Simon would never have been raised. Those who teach that a believer cannot be lost were confronted with the fact that Simon, after he was baptized, was said to have fallen under condemnation. To save their doctrine, they must declare that Simon was never saved! Even if Simon could have deceived Philip he could not have deceived Jehovah; and Luke, writing by inspiration of the Holy Spirit, said that Simon believed. If Simon did not believe, then we cannot believe the plain statement of God. Is it not strange that a professed believer in God, simply to sustain his doctrine, will virtually accuse God of making misleading statements about Simon? God says: "He that believeth and is baptized shall be saved," and the authors of this book believe it. He also said Simon believed and was baptized, and we believe that; and if we did not believe what God said about Simon having believed we would feel that our condition was about on a par with Simon's when later he sinned and Peter said: "Thou are in the gall of bitterness and in the bond of iniquity."

PETER AND JOHN SENT TO SAMARIA.

"Now when the apostles that were at Jerusalem heard that Samaria had received the word of God, they sent unto them Peter and John: who, when they were come down, prayed for them, that they might receive the Holy Spirit: for as yet he was fallen upon none of them: only they had been baptized in the name of the

Lord Jesus. Then laid they their hands on them, and they received the Holy Spirit" (vs. 14-17). "Whatever other purpose may have prompted the mission of the two apostles, such as confirming the faith of the disciples or assisting Philip in his labors, it is quite certain that the chief purpose was the impartation of the Holy Spirit. What they did on their arrival was certainly that for which they went; but the chief thing which they did was to confer the Holy Spirit; therefore, this was the chief purpose of their visit."—McGarvey. At least it would seem that what they did on their arrival was that for which they came. But this miraculous endowment of the Spirit was not necessary to the remission of sins, nor membership in the church, for these disciples enjoyed both these blessings, having been "baptized into the name of the Lord Jesus."

WHY THE MIRACULOUS ENDOWMENT?

The apostles were baptized in the Holy Spirit that they might be able to preach the gospel to all people, and perform signs to confirm the word, and give the world, through their writings, a full revelation of God's will. But the complete revelation was not full written out for about three-quarters of a century after the gospel was first preached. The apostles could not be present with every church, and the New Testament had not been written. What, then, would the church do for guidance? To meet this need certain persons in the different congregations were miraculously endowed, some having one gift and some another. Paul's discussion of these gifts may be found in the twelfth, thirteenth, and fourteenth chapters of First Corinthians. In a later volume we will discuss this matter fully.

SIMON'S SIN.

"Now when Simon saw that through the laying on of the apostle's hands the Holy Spirit was given, he offered them money, saying, Give me also this power, that on whomsoever I lay my hands, he may receive the Holy Spirit" (vs. 18, 19). Be it observed that Simon did not offer money for the miraculous power conferred by Peter and John, but for the power to impart this miraculous power to others by laying on his hands as Peter and John had done. A man's mode of living and thinking leave their impress on his character, and even after he turns from them he is likely to fall into his old error under strong temptation. Simon had gained money and notoriety through tricks of sorcery. Now a new field seems to be open to him, in which he could gain even more money and greater notoriety. He offered them money. But Peter, without an effort to use soft words, promptly replied: "Thy silver perish with thee, because thou hast thought to obtain the gift of God with money. Thou hast neither part nor lot in this matter: for thy heart is not right before God. Repent therefore of this thy wickedness, and pray the Lord, if perhaps the thought of thy heart shall be forgiven thee. For I see that thou are in the gall of bitterness and in the bond of iniquity" (vs. 20-23). Peter charges only one sin against him—the desire to purchase the gift of God with money—and he called on him to repent of only one sin—"this thy wickedness." Had he not been forgiven of his old sins, Peter's speech would have been misleading, for Peter certainly gave him to understand that he needed to repent of only one sin. But this sin was so grievous as to bring him into the "gall of bitterness" and into the "bond of iniquity." Certainly Simon expected no such reply from Peter; and though it drove to the heart like a pointed shaft, he did not resent it. In fear he said: "Pray ye for me to the Lord, that none of these things which ye have spoken come upon me" (v. 24). Who can doubt for a moment that Peter did pray for him, or doubt God's willingness to forgive?

What course of life Simon followed after this is a mere matter of conjecture.

THE TWO LAWS OF PARDON.

That the child of God who sins and the alien sinner stand in different relationships to God is apparent to any thoughtful person; one is outside the family of God, the other is an erring child. To the alien, those outside the family, outside the kingdom, Peter said: "Repent ye, and be baptized every one of you in the name of Jesus Christ unto the remission of your sins" (Acts 2: 38). This is part of what one must do to become a child of God. If the child sins, what then? The case of Simon gives the answer. To him, as an erring child, Peter said: "Repent therefore of this thy wickedness, and pray the Lord."

* * *

TOPICS FOR INVESTIGATION AND DISCUSSION.

1. Laying on Hands.
2. Magicians and Familiar Spirits.
3. Have Miracles Ceased?
4. Our Attitude Toward Members of Church Who Sin?
5. Our Duty in Preaching the Word.

* * *

QUESTIONS.

1. Where is Samaria?
2. By whom was the city of Samaria founded?
3. Who were the Samaritans?
4. What their religion?
5. What feeling existed between the Samaritans and Jews?
6. Were the Samaritans hospitable toward Christ?
7. In what city was the gospel first preached?
8. What success attended the preaching?

9. What the immediate cause of its being preached elsewhere?
10. To what extent was the Jerusalem church scattered?
11. What did the scattered church do?
12. What is meant by evangelizing?
13. Can one evangelize without making public speeches?
14. Is traveling necessary to evangelizing?
15. When is Philip first mentioned?
16. What his first work?
17. Why did his work as a deacon cease?
18. When driven from Jerusalem, where did Philip go?
19. What did Philip preach?
20. What the burden of God's inspired preachers?
21. Under what commission was Philip preaching?
22. Prove that preaching Christ, the gospel, and the word are the same.
23. How was Moses preached?
24. Name some of the titles of Christ.
25. Name a title showing his relationship to man.
26. Name a title showing his relationship to God.
27. What is involved in fully preaching Christ?
28. Show that one cannot preach Christ and let others alone.
29. What is a prophet?
30. What is a priest, and what his functions?
31. What is involved in preaching Christ as King?
32. What did the Samaritans believe?
33. Do men boldly preach Christ today?
34. What results attended Philip's preaching?
35. What the purpose of the miracles of Philip?
36. What wonder worker was in Samaria?
37. How did the people regard him?
38. What the difference between the wonders of Simon and the works wrought through Philip?
39. What did the Samaritans do when they believed Philip's preaching?
40. Who was baptized?
41. Show that the record harmonizes with the Great Commission.
42. What produced faith of the Samaritans?
43. What led them to be baptized?
44. Were there any infants in the number baptized?
45. Is there a record of infant baptism in the Bible?

CONVERSION OF THE SAMARITANS

46. Who voted on the Samaritans to see if they should be baptized?
47. What did Simon do when he heard Philip's preaching?
48. Was Simon saved? Proof.
49. Why do some try to prove that Simon was not saved?
50. Who said Simon believed?
51. Is the witness trustworthy?
52. Who said he was baptized?
53. Why did Peter and John go to Samaria?
54. What did they do on arriving in Samaria?
55. Was their visit necessary to the salvation of the Samaritans?
56. What the purpose of the miraculous endowment of the Holy Spirit?
57. Why did the church in Samaria need the endowment of the Spirit?
58. Did Simon receive the Spirit?
59. What proposition did Simon make to the apostles?
60. What kind of temptation would appeal most strongly to Simon?
61. What did Peter reply to Simon?
62. Of how many sins did Peter accuse Simon?
63. In what condition, or state, did Simon's sin place him?
64. What did Peter tell Simon to do?
65. What request did Simon make of Peter?
66. What the difference between an alien sinner and an erring child?
67. Discuss the two laws of pardon.

FAITH.

LESSON TEXT: Heb. 11:1-30.
MEMORY VERSES: James 2:14-24.

Faith is sometimes defined as the belief of a proposition supported by testimony. This is true with reference to facts and things. You believe the Kaiser was driven from his throne, and that there is a city in Italy called "Rome;" but faith in a person means more than to just believe that such a man lived. Frequently one says: "I believe in that man, because I know him." Here faith contains an element of trust, or confidence. To believe in your physician is to have confidence in him, and you show your confidence in him by committing your case into his hands and doing what he says. To believe in God is to commit ourselves, our ways, into his hands and to diligently follow his directions.

CAIN AND ABEL.

Cain believed in the existence of Jehovah, and made an offering to him, but instead of offering the thing commanded, he trusted to his own wisdom and offered of the first-fruits of the ground (see Gen. 4:1). But Abel showed his faith, his confidence in Jehovah, by doing what he said.

MOSES.

On one occasion Moses failed to trust God. "Moses lifted up his hand, and smote the rock with his rod twice: and water came forth abundantly, and the congregation drank, and their cattle. And Jehovah said unto Moses and Aaron, Because ye believed not in me, to sanctify me in the eyes of the children of Israel, therefore ye shall not bring this assembly into the land which I have given them" (Num. 20:11, 12). Now Moses certainly believed in the existence of God; but his overconfidence in self and lack of confidence in Jehovah led him to adopt his own way instead of the Lord's and God said: "Because ye believed not in me."

WHY FAILURE TO OBEY?

Only one of three things could cause a person to fail to follow the directions of his physician: (1) Inability to do so; (2) failure to understand him; or (3) a lack of confidence in him. The same is true of our obeying God. But we can do what he says, for God requires no impossibilities. And as we have God's revealed will, it is not necessary to disobey through ignorance. Your disobedience is attributable to, lack of confidence in Jehovah.

To set aside the physician's directions is to take the case in your own hands, to become your own physician. To set aside God's directions for your salvation is to take the matter out of his hands and become your own savior. What we need is full confidence in God's love, mercy, grace, and wisdom. This would eliminate all desires to depart from his way.

FAITH IN MEN AND INSTITUTIONS.

Faith is essential in all the relationships of life. Business is conducted, and credit is extended, on the basis of faith. Should we lose confidence in our financial institutions, withdraw our money from the banks, and refuse to extend credit, chaos would follow. An element of faith enters into all our business transactions. Our social relations are based on faith. There can be no satisfactory association with another without faith. Men have faith in their wives, wives believe in their husbands. Destroy this faith and the home is ruined.

Harmony with God is necessary to salvation, and there can be no harmony, no walking with God, without a whole-hearted faith in him. A lack of faith in God has been the cause of all the departures, sin, and disobedience of all ages. "Take heed, brethren, lest haply there shall be in any one of you an evil heart and unbelief, in falling away from the living God" (Heb. 3:12).

FAITH ESSENTIAL TO SALVATION.

That faith is necessary to salvation is hardly questioned by those who profess to believe the Bible. Faith is clearly demanded as a condition of salvation.

"He that believeth not shall be damned" (Mark 16:16).

"Without faith it is impossible to be well-pleasing unto him; for he that cometh to God must believe that he is, and that he is a rewarder of them that seek after him" (Heb. 11:6).

"Sirs, what must I do to be saved? And they said, Believe on the Lord Jesus, and thou shalt be saved, thou and thy house" (Acts 16:30, 31; see Heb. 10:39; Rom. 13:11; I Cor. 1:21).

WHAT MUST ONE BELIEVE?

You must believe certain things to become a Methodist, and certain other things to become a Baptist, and still other things to become a Presbyterian. The Methodist declares that the man who is a Baptist will be saved, though he does not believe the peculiar things one must believe to become a Methodist. In making such a declaration the Methodist clearly declares that the things peculiar to Methodism are not necessary to salvation. The Methodists, Baptists, and Presbyterians concede that the things peculiar to their respective churches, things which one must believe to become a member of their respective churches, are not necessary to salvation. It must follow, then, that it is not necessary for one to believe the peculiar doctrines of these churches unless it is desired to become a member of the particular church. Methodists, Baptists, and Presbyterians insist that one can be saved without being in either of their respective churches. This is a free admission that belief of their peculiar doctrines is not necessary to salvation.

Since it is not necessary to believe the distinctive doctrines of Methodists, Baptists, or Presbyterians to be saved, what must one believe?

ONE MUST BELIEVE IN CHRIST.

"Sirs, what must I do to be saved? And they said, Believe on the Lord Jesus, and thou shalt be saved, thou and thy house" (Acts 16: 30, 31).

"Many other signs therefore did Jesus in the presence of his disciples, which are not written in this book: but these are written, that ye may believe that Jesus is the Christ, the Son of God; and that believing ye may have life in his name" (John 20: 30, 31).

"If thou shalt confess with thy mouth Jesus as Lord, and shalt believe in thy heart that God raised him from the dead, thou shall be saved" (Rom. 10:9).

"And this is the victory that hath overcome the world, even our faith. And who is he that overcometh the world, but he that believeth that Jesus is the Son of God" (I John 5:4, 5).

HOW DOES FAITH COME?

Faith is the result of testimony. If you wish one to believe a proposition, it is necessary for the evidence to be submitted to that person, attesting the truthfulness of the proposition to be believed. The evidence may be presented orally or in writing.

WRITTEN EVIDENCE. "Many other signs therefore did

Jesus in the presence of his disciples, which are not written in this book: but these are written, that ye may believe that Jesus is the Christ, the Son of God; and that believing ye may have life in his name" (John 20: 30, 31). "Now these were more noble than those in Thessalonica, in that they received the word with all readiness of mind, examining the scriptures daily, whether these things were so. Many of them therefore believed; also of the Greek women of honorable estate, and of men, not a few" (Acts 17:11, 12).

ORAL TESTIMONY. "How then shall they call on him in whom they have not believed? and how shall they believe in him whom they have not heard? and how shall they hear without a preacher?... So belief cometh by hearing, and hearing by the word of Christ" (Rom. 10:14-17). "Ye know that a good while ago God made choice among you, that by my mouth the Gentiles should hear the word of the gospel, and believe" (Acts 15:7).

DEGREES OF FAITH.

There is one faith (Eph. 4:4), but this one faith may exist in different degrees. All have not the same degree of faith, as is evidenced by the Bible.

LITTLE FAITH. "O ye of little faith" (Matt. 8:26).

GREAT FAITH. "I have not found so great faith, no not in Israel" (Matt. 8:10).

WEAK FAITH. "Him that is weak in faith" (Rom. 14:1).

STRONG FAITH. Abraham "waxed strong through faith" (Rom. 4:20).

DEAD FAITH. "Faith apart from works is dead" (James 2:26).

PERFECT FAITH. "By works was faith made perfect" (James 2:22).

BELIEVE WITH ALL THE HEART.

To believe with all the heart is more than to give intellectual assent to the truthfulness of a proposition. The heart includes the intellect, the emotions, and the will. With the heart we think (Matt. 9:4), reason (Mark 2:6), understand (Isa. 32:4). These processes are purely intellectual. With the heart we sorrow (Neh. 2:2), despise (II Sam. 6:16), love (Matt. 22:37). These are emotional processes. With the heart we purpose (II Cor. 9:7). This is a determining process. To believe with all the heart involves all of these. You accept many things as true which do not involve either the emotions or the will. You believe that the Pharaohs ruled in Egypt, but you never love them nor are you determined to serve them. You do not believe it with all your heart. Many believe in God and Jesus Christ, his Son, in the same way. They have no doubt of Jehovah's existence, but they neither love him nor are they determined to serve him. They do not believe with all their heart. If one believes with all the heart, he will serve.

Frequently one hears the statement: "Mr. X believes as strong as you, but, for some cause, he will not obey." Such a statement is not true, for the degree of one's faith is shown by the services rendered. In the mind of Neighbor X there may not be a doubt as to the truthfulness of certain doctrines, or all that Jesus said. Such is commendable as far as it goes. You should remember, though, the intellect is not all the heart; his faith must include his emotions and his will—that is, he must have involved his whole heart, which will give his love and service to the Master. The demons believed (James 2:19), but they neither loved God nor were they determined to serve him. They did not believe with all the heart, neither does your disobedient neighbor. "If a man love me, he will keep my word" (John 14:

23). "If you love me, ye will keep my commandments" (John 14:15). "He that loveth me not keepeth not my words" (John 14:24).

Faith that does not involve the will so as to control the life never benefited a son or daughter of Adam.

SALVATION IS NOT BY FAITH ONLY.

That we are saved by faith no one doubts. But some contend that we are saved by faith only—that is, that we are saved the very moment we believe. In the Discipline of the Methodist Episcopal, Church, South, Article IX., the doctrine is avowed in these words: "Wherefore that we are justified by faith only is a most wholesome doctrine, and very full of comfort."

BY FAITH ONLY.	NOT BY FAITH ONLY.
"We are justified by faith only." — M. E. Discipline, Art. IX.	"By works a man is justified, and not by faith only" (James 2:24).

Does it seem strange to you that any one would teach a doctrine which in such plain terms contradicts the Bible?

BELIEVERS GIVEN POWER TO BECOME SONS.

"He came unto his own, and they that were his own received him not. But as many as received him, to them gave he the right to become children of God, even to them that believed on his name" (John 1:11, 12). He gave the believers the right to become the children of God. (1) Believed; (2) given right to (3) become children of God. If one is saved the moment he believes, he is saved before he becomes a child of God, for the believer is given the right to become the child.

SAVED WITHOUT THE NEW BIRTH?

It one is saved the moment he believes, he is saved without the new birth. Believers are given the "right to become the children of God." It must be evident, then, that if one is saved the moment he believes, he is saved before he becomes a child of God; and if saved before he becomes a child of God, he is saved without being born again, for one cannot be born again without in the birth becoming a child of God.

SAVED BY IMPERFECT FAITH?

If one is saved the moment he believes, he is saved by an imperfect faith. "Thou seest that faith wrought with his works, and by works was faith made perfect" (James 2:22). Are you prepared to contend that man is saved by an imperfect faith? He who contends that man is saved the moment he believes claims salvation by an imperfect faith, for "by works was faith made perfect." Of course you understand that faith must exist before it can work, and till it works it is not perfect; and if salvation is by faith before it works, it is salvation by an imperfect faith.

SALVATION BY DEAD FAITH?

If one is saved the moment he believes, if he is saved by "faith only," he is saved by "faith apart from works," and that would be salvation by a dead faith. "As the body without the spirit is dead, even so faith apart from works is dead" (James 2:26). The body, when the spirit has left it, is dead; it is worthless so far as blessing man is concerned. Just so it is with faith apart from works—"faith apart from works is dead." The dead faith—faith apart from works—can no more bless man than can the body without the spirit bless men.

SAVED WITHOUT CONFESSING?

If one is saved the moment he believes, he is saved without the necessity of loving God's praise, or confessing him.

"Nevertheless even of the rulers many believed on him; but because of the Pharisees they did not confess it, lest they should be put out of the synagogue: for they loved the glory that is of men more than the glory that is of God" (John 12:42, 43). These cowardly rulers believed—that is plainly stated—but they refused to confess it. Do you tell us that God will save a man who is too cowardly to confess it, ashamed to confess Christ, a man who loves the glory that is of men more than he loves the glory that is of God? Though these rulers believed, they would not confess. They had "faith only;" and if one is saved by "faith only," if one is saved the moment he believes, the rulers were saved. Do you insist that one is saved without confessing Christ? I understand that "faith only" does not include confessing Christ. But are men saved who refuse to confess Christ? Men must believe before they can confess Christ, and men must confess Christ to be saved: "For with the heart man believeth unto righteousness; and with the mouth confession is made unto salvation" (Rom. 10:9, 10). Are people saved who refuse to confess Christ?

FAITH ONLY WILL NOT AVAIL.

If one is saved the moment he believes; if one is saved by "faith only," then faith only avails, whereas God declares that "faith only" does not avail. "For in Christ Jesus neither circumcision availeth anything, nor uncircumcision; but faith which worketh by love" (Gal. 5:6). (1) Circumcision does not avail. (2) Uncircumcision does not avail. (3) But faith which works by love does avail. (4) Faith must exist before it can work. (5) Faith must work before it avails. (6) It must follow that faith alone, "faith only," cannot avail, for "faith only" is faith without works.

FAITH ONLY DOES NOT PROFIT.

"What doth it profit, my brethren, if a man say he hath faith, but have not works? can that faith save him?" (James 2:14). Again: "If a brother or sister be naked and in lack of daily food, and one of you say unto them, Go in peace, be ye warmed and filled; and yet ye give not them the things needful to the body; what doth it profit? Even so faith, if it have not works, is dead in itself" (James 2:15-17). This should settle the matter with every unbiased student. "Faith only" can profit one no more than saying to the hungry, "Go in peace, be ye warmed and filled," when not a mouthful is given to eat; or to say to the naked, "Be ye warmed," when not a thing in the form of clothing is supplied.

SAVED AND NOT PARDONED?

If one is saved the moment he believes, he is saved before he turns to the Lord; and if saved before he turns to the Lord, he is saved before he is pardoned.

Men must believe before they turn to the Lord. "And the hand of the Lord was with them: and a great number that believed turned unto the Lord" (Acts 11:21). (1) Believed and (2) turned unto the Lord. Clearly, after they believed, they "turned unto the Lord." Is one saved before he "turns unto the Lord?" "Let the wicked forsake his way, and the unrighteous man his thoughts; and let him return unto Jehovah, and he will have mercy upon him; and to our God, for he will abundantly pardon" (Isa. 55:7). Men must turn unto the Lord before he pardons them, but they believe before they turn. If one is saved the moment he believes, he is saved before he turns; and if saved before he turns, he is saved before he is pardoned.

God has never saved a man on the condition of faith till that faith has expressed itself in some act.

TOPICS FOR INVESTIGATION AND DISCUSSION.

1. Can an alien sinner believe?
2. Opinion, Faith, Knowledge.
3. Faithful men.
4. Walking by faith.
5. Faith in social and business world.

* * *

QUESTIONS ON FAITH.

1. What is faith?
2. Show how true faith has in it an element of confidence and trust.
3. Discuss the points illustrated by the case of Cain and Abel.
4. Why did Jehovah say to Moses and Aaron: "Ye believe not in me?"
5. Why do sick men refuse to follow the directions of the physician?
6. Why do people fail to follow the direction of the Great Physician?
7. Show how business transactions are based on faith.
8. Show that faith is necessary in the social life.
9. Show that we cannot be at peace with God without faith.
10. Prove that faith is essential to salvation.
11. Do all denominations teach some things that one must believe to be saved?
12. Show by the admission of denominations that it is not necessary to salvation to believe the things peculiar to them.
13. What, then, must one believe? Give references.
14. How does faith come?
15. What the difference, if any, between faith and belief?
16. Is there a distinction between written and oral testimony?
17. Illustrate degrees of faith.
18. What is meant by the heart?
19. Illustrate the difference between the intellectual, emotional, and determining functions of the heart.
20. What is it to believe with all the heart?
21. Do we believe every proposition with all the heart?

FAITH

22. What does a man do when he believes in Christ with all the heart?
23. Do the disobedient believe with all the heart?
24. What was the character of faith of demons? (James 2:19).
25. What does James say about justification by "faith only?"
26. What does the M. E. Discipline say about justification by "faith only?"
27. Quote and discuss John 1: 11, 12.
28. Show that if one is saved the moment he believes he is saved without the new birth.
29. Will an imperfect faith save?
30. How is faith made perfect?
31. What is a dead faith?
32. Show that dead faith cannot bless.
33. Discuss the faith of the rulers, and show it does not save.
34. Show that faith only does not avail.
35. Show by the discussion in James that faith only does not profit.
36. Show that if one is saved the moment he believes, he is saved and not pardoned.
37. Can you give an example where God blessed a man on the condition of his faith before that faith expressed itself in some act?

JUSTIFICATION BY FAITH.

"Being therefore justified by faith, we have peace with God through our Lord Jesus Christ" (Rom. 5:1). Had Paul said we are justified "by faith only," he would have contradicted James, who said: "By works a man is justified, and not by faith only" (James 2:24). Some people think they believe the doctrine of justification by faith only, but in reality they do not. Ask a defender of the doctrine of "justification by faith only" these questions: Do you believe a person can be saved without repentance? Do you believe a person can be saved without prayer? Do you believe a person can be saved without love? He will answer with an emphatic "No." But if one must believe, repent, pray, and love, he is not justified by "faith only." If you can add repentance, prayer, and love to faith, and it still be "faith only," could you not add anything else God commands, and still have "faith only?" If faith without repentance, prayer, and love will not save, then "faith only" does not save.

DEGREES OF FAITH. In the previous lesson we found that faith may, and does, exist in different degrees. Faith without work is dead, and therefore worthless. It is dead because it has no connection with God, the source of life. But faith, when made perfect by works, is a living faith, because by obedience it is brought into vital connection with God. Evidently it is this degree of faith by which Paul declares we are justified. Bearing this in mind, it will be seen that there is no lack of harmony between Paul and James.

"BY FAITH." How can we determine the meaning of "by faith?" If there is any doubt as to the meaning an author attaches to any word or phrase in a given place, a clear understanding may be reached by carefully studying the use he makes of it in all his writings. Now, it so happens that Paul makes frequent use of the phase "by faith." It should be, and is, an easy matter to determine exactly what is meant by this phrase in his writings, for in many places he uses the term in such connection as to leave no room for doubt as to his meaning. "By faith" occurs many times in the eleventh chapter of Hebrews; the student should read that chapter carefully. We call attention to some of the examples therein mentioned as illustrative of the meaning of "by faith."

EXAMPLES.

ABEL. "By faith Abel offered unto God a more excellent sacrifice than Cain, through which he had witness born to him that he was righteous, God bearing witness in respect of his gifts: and through it he being dead yet speaketh" (Heb. 11:4). Evidently Abel did not offer a sacrifice by "faith only;" yet it is as emphatically affirmed that he offered a sacrifice "by faith" as it is that we are justified "by faith." What was embraced in the term "by faith" in the sacrifice offered by Abel? We are not advised as to how long it took Abel to prepare the altar and the sacrifice; but we do know that whether the time was long or short the phrase "by faith" covers every move he made and every lick he struck in building the altar and offering the sacrifice. In this case, then, we know that the phrase "by faith" does not mean "faith only."

NOAH AND THE ARK. "By faith Noah, being warned of God concerning things not seen as yet, moved with godly fear, prepared an ark to the saving of his house; through which he condemned the world, and become heir of the righteousness which is according to faith" (Heb. 11:7). We do not know how long it took Noah to build the ark. The one hundred and twenty years mentioned in Gen. 6:3 was the time of respite given the people after Jehovah decided to destroy them (see "Sound Doctrine," Vol. I., page 42). But whether it required ten years or five years to build the ark, this we know: that every step he took, every move he made, and every lick he struck in felling the trees, collecting the material, and putting it together, is included in the phrase "by faith." The ark was built "by faith;" so are we justified "by faith." Think of the days of toil spent in building the ark and know that the phrase "by faith" does not mean by "faith only." The finished ark was the result of Noah's faith. So when the Christian reaches heaven, though he may have served God faithfully for three score years, it may be truly said that he is there "by faith."

ABRAHAM'S CALL. "By faith Abraham, when he was called, obeyed to go out unto a place which he was to receive for an inheritance; and he went out, not knowing whither he went" (Heb. 11:8). Abraham's faith took him from his home in Ur of the Chaldees to the far distant land of Canaan. When God spoke, Abraham's faith obeyed, and thus he became the father of the faithful, the father of all those who walk in the steps of Abraham (Rom. 4:12). Hence, the phrase "by faith" includes every step from Ur of Canaan.

ABRAHAM OFFERED ISAAC BY FAITH. "By faith Abraham, being tried, offered up Isaac: yea, he that had gladly received the promises was offering up his only begotten son; even he to whom it was said, In Isaac shall thy seed be called" (Heb. 11:17, 18). A full account of this is given in Gen. 22:1-19. Abraham offered up Isaac by faith—we are justified by faith. Certainly no one will contend that Abraham offered up Isaac by "faith only;" yet the same phrase, "by faith;" is used here as in Rom. 5:1. Read the account of this offering as given in Genesis, and see what is included in the phrase "by faith" in this case. Jehovah commanded Abraham to take Isaac and to go into the land of Moriah "and offer him for a burnt offering upon one of the mountains which I will tell thee of." Abraham made the necessary preparations, and with Isaac departed to go unto the place to be shown him. On the third day he saw the place afar off. Abraham and Isaac climbed the mountain, the altar was prepared, the wood was placed in order upon the altar, Isaac was bound and laid upon the altar, and Abraham lifted the knife to slay the son. All this is included in the phrase "by faith" in this reference. "By faith" in this reference included the three days of active, heart-rending service.

MOSES AND THE PASSOVER. "By faith he kept the passover, and the sprinkling of the blood, that the destroyer of the firstborn should not touch them" (Heb. 11:28). Kept the passover "by faith"—justified "by faith." Unless it can be shown that Moses kept the passover by faith only, why should it be contended that we are justified by faith only? To keep the passover by faith required more than the simple act of believing in God. In this instance, "by faith" includes what? A full account is given in the twelfth chapter of Exodus. On the tenth day of the first month they put up the lamb, on the fourteenth day they killed and roasted it, and on the night of the fifteenth day they ate the lamb with bitter herbs. All these services, all these acts of obedience, are here included in the phrase "by faith."

THE WALLS OF JERICHO. "By faith the walls of Jericho fell down, after they had been compassed about for seven days" (Heb. 11:30). Here is what was done: "And Joshua rose early in the morning, and the priests took up the ark of Jehovah. And the seven priests bearing the seven trumpets of rams' horns before the ark of Jehovah went on continually, and blew the trumpets:

and the armed men went before them; and the rearward came after the ark of Jehovah, the priests blowing the trumpets as they went. And the second day they compassed the city once, and returned into the camp: so they did six days. And in came to pass on the seventh day, that they arose early at the dawning of the day, and compassed the city after the same manner seven times: only on that day they compassed the city seven times. And it came to pass at the seventh time, when the priests blew the trumpets, Joshua said unto the people, Shout; for Jehovah hath given you the city..... So the people shouted, and the priests blew the trumpets: and it came to pass, when the people heard the sound of the trumpet, that the people shouted with a great shout, and the walls fell down flat, so that the people went up into the city, every man straight before him, and they took the city" (Josh. 6:12-20). Did the walls fall down by "faith only?" Yet it is just as plainly said that the walls fell down "by faith" as it is that we are justified "by faith." Their faith led them to do what God commanded, and was thus perfected by works, and by this perfect faith the walls fell down. If we would be justified "by faith," our faith must be strong enough to lead us to do what God commands; by this perfect faith we are justified.

"BY FAITH," THEN, INCLUDES WHAT?

In every case the phrase "by faith" includes obedience to all the things commanded. "Perfect faith is taking God at his word, and doing what he says." Is not that a good definition? Is it not true? Try substituting this definition in a few of the examples found in the eleventh chapter of Hebrews. By taking God at his word and doing what he said Noah built the ark. By taking God at his word and doing what he said Abraham offered up Isaac. By taking God at his word and doing what he said they kept the passover. And by taking God at his word and doing what he says we are justified. Certainly if we did not take God at his word and do what he says we would not be justified.

Thus it will be seen that faith in every instance includes whatever acts of obedience God had commanded in that particular case. This is faith made perfect by works, the faith by which we are justified.

THE FINAL EXAMPLE. "By faith they passed through the Red Sea as by dry land: which the Egyptians assaying to do were swallowed up" (Heb. 11:29). They crossed the Red Sea "by faith," but they were not on the other side the moment they believed. They spent a night of anxious toil and great fear before they could sing the song of deliverance on the other side. Here the phrase "by faith" spans the Red Sea, and includes every step they took in crossing.

By some it is thought that because Paul says we are justified by faith baptism is excluded. But in the examples so far considered the phrase "by faith," instead of excluding the acts of faith, which, in reality, make faith perfect, actually includes obedience. And it can be plainly shown that "by faith" in this case includes baptism. Paul says: "For I would not, brethren, have you ignorant, that our fathers were all under the cloud, and all passed through the sea; and were all baptized unto Moses in the cluod and in the sea" (I Cor. 10:1, 2). They crossed the Red Sea by faith, and in crossing they were baptized. "By faith" includes what was done in crossing. But in crossing they were baptized. Therefore, "by faith," in this example, includes baptism. From this conclusion there is no escape.

By many this is thought to be a type of our deliverance from sin. If so, then as baptism is in the phrase "by faith," it must be in the phrase "by faith" in the antitype. But does "by faith," in the matter of our becoming Christians, really include baptism? One plain statement from Paul settles it: "For ye are all the sons of God, through faith, in Christ Jesus." On what grounds did he affirm that they were sons of God by faith? He settles all doubt by immediately adding: "For as many of you as were baptized into Christ did put on Christ" (see Gal. 3:26, 27). Paul here affirmed that they were children of God by faith, because they had been baptized into Christ. Certainly no one will contend that had they refused to be baptized their faith would have made them sons of God.

JUSTIFIED BY FAITH, WE HAVE PEACE.

That we are justified "by faith" is not a question for discussion amongst those who believe the Bible, for it is plainly declared. The only question that can be raised is: "When are we justified by faith?" Paul declares that when we are justified "by faith" we have "peace." When journeying along the highway enroute to Damascus to bind Christians and thrust them into prison, Paul was struck blind, and cried to the Lord: "What wilt thou have me to do?" The Lord told him to go to the city and there it would be told him what he must do. Immediately Paul journeyed to the city, as the Lord directed, and thereby evidenced the fact that he had faith in the Lord. Was he justified "by faith" at the time he arose and walked toward the city? Did he have "peace" at that time? See him in the city; he is blind, without food and without drink for three days, and praying at least some of the time. Do you think a man in that condition has "peace?" In the city, suffering from the loss of his sight, abstaining from food, with goading conscience, filled with sorrow over the life he had lived in persecuting Jesus, and wasting the church of God, he is praying to know what to do. Certainly peace has not yet come to him. To him the Lord sent Ananias.

who instructed him to be baptized and wash away his sins (see Acts 22:16). His faith promptly obeyed, and, his sins now being forgiven, he takes food. The period of mourning is over. He is now justified by faith, and has peace with God.

If possible, let the teacher have the following outline on the blackboard, to be used during the recitation of this lesson:

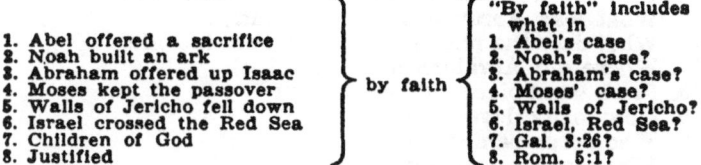

1. Abel offered a sacrifice
2. Noah built an ark
3. Abraham offered up Isaac
4. Moses kept the passover
5. Walls of Jericho fell down
6. Israel crossed the Red Sea
7. Children of God
8. Justified

} by faith {

"By faith" includes what in
1. Abel's case
2. Noah's case?
3. Abraham's case?
4. Moses' case?
5. Walls of Jericho?
6. Israel, Red Sea?
7. Gal. 3:26?
8. Rom. 5:1?

There is not an instance where "by faith" means "faith only."

* * *

TOPICS FOR INVESTIGATION AND DISCUSSION.
1. Walking by Faith.
2. Abraham as an Example of Faith.
3. Paul as an Example of Faith.
4. Wherein We Are Defective in Faith.
5. Consolations and Rewards of Faith.

* * *

QUESTIONS

1. What passage does the doctrine of justification by "faith only" contradict?
2. What is a dead faith?
3. How is faith made perfect?
4. What kind of sacrifice were Cain and Abel commanded to bring?
5. Abel's sacrifice was "by faith"—what does "by faith" include in this case?
6. Of what kind of wood was the ark built?

7. Would another kind of wood have met the demands of God?
8. Give a case where a substitution was made for what God commanded, and tell the results.
9. How many stories were in the ark? Windows? Doors?
10. How many animals, clean and unclean?
11. Name some of the unclean animals.
12. How long was Noah building the ark
13. What does "by faith" include in the building of the ark?
14. How old was Abraham when God called him?
15. What was Abraham's native country?
16. What does the phrase "by faith" here include?
17. Where did Abraham offer Isaac?
18. From what place did he journey?
19. How many days' journey?
20. Who accompanied him?
21. Who saw the sacrifice?
22. What does "by faith" include in the offering of Isaac?
23. When was the passover instituted?
24. Why?
25. What elements were used in the passover?
26. What day of the month were they required to put up the animal?
27. When was the animal killed?
28. When—what day of the month — did they eat the animal?
29. What does "by faith" include in the observance of the passover?
30. In what country was Jericho?
31. Tell all you know about that city.
32. Who was leading Israel when they took Jericho?
33. What the order of procession around the walls?
34. Who bore the ark?
35. Where was the ark builded?
36. Who was in the ark?
37. Describe the ark.
38. How many days did they march around the city? How many times?
39. When the last journey around the city was made, what was done?
40. Did the walls fall "by faith?"
41. What does "by faith" include in this case?
42. Where is the Red Sea?

JUSTIFICATION BY FAITH

43. What did Israel say when they were on the bank of the sea?
44. What did Paul say to Israel when they were crossing the sea, in I Cor. 10:1, 2?
45. What did God do for Israel the day they crossed the sea (Ex. 14:30)?
46. How did God protect them as they crossed the sea?
47. What happened to the Egyptians?
48. When did the Israelites sing songs of deliverance?
49. Paul says: "By faith they crossed the Red Sea." Can "by faith" in this case means "faith only?"
50. Show that the phrase "by faith" includes baptism.
51. On what grounds did Paul declare that the Galatians were children of God by faith?
52. Rom. 5:1: We are justified "by faith." What does "by faith" in this passage include?
53. When did Paul have peace with God?

REPENTANCE.

LESSON TEXT: Luke 13:3-14.
MEMORY VERSE: II Cor. 7:10.

Sin is found wherever man abides.

Christ not only designed to save man from sin, but to save him from the penalty of sin as well.

"Sin is lawlessness" (I John 3:4).

Jehovah, our Creator, gave a law to govern man. A low without a penalty is no law. If a law is just and the penalty equitable, it is right to inflict the penalty on the transgressor. The "lawless" man should be punished.

"The law of the Lord is perfect, restoring the soul" (Psa. 19:7). It is not the province of the creature to make the laws to govern himself. "It is not in man that walketh to direct his steps" (Jer. 10:23). Man transgressed the law of the Lord and justice declared it right to execute the law. Law has no mercy. The law says the same thing so long as it is in force. Mercy may be extended to the condemned by the one who has the right, but the law which condemned does not extend mercy.

Jehovah has always desired the salvation of the lost, "not wishing that any should perish, but that all should come to repentance" (II Peter 3:9) and obtain the mercy he extends. To enjoy the salvation he offers, one must repent.

Throughout the Old Testament ages men were required to repent, and it was necessary for them to comply with this law of Jehovah if they would enjoy his favor.

THE PREACHING OF JOHN THE BAPTIST.

John the Baptist denounced sin, and called on the people to repent. "John came, who baptized in the wilderness and preached the baptism of repentance unto remission of sins" (Mark 1:4), saying, "Ye offspring of vipers, who warned you to flee from the wrath to come? Bring forth therefore fruit worthy of repentance" (Matt. 3:7, 8). "Repent ye; for the kingdom of heaven is at hand" (Matt. 3:2).

JESUS PREACHED REPENTANCE.

The minstry of Jesus is marked by the constant cry of repentance. "Repent ye, and believe in the gospel" (Mark 1:15). "Except ye repent, ye shall all in like manner perish" (Luke 13:3). In the Great Commission the Lord demands that people repent (Luke 24:46-49), and the apostles faithfully preached repentance: "Repent ye, and be baptized" (Acts 2:38). "Repent ye therefore, and turn again" (Acts 3:19). "He commandeth men that they should all everywhere repent" (Acts 17:30). "Then to the Gentiles also hath God granted repentance unto life" (Acts 11:18).

Repentance being a command from God, being necessary to life, a condition of the remission of sins, it is important, therefore, that one know what repentance is, else he may never know that he has repented.

REPENTANCE IS NOT SORROW FOR SIN.

Should you call for an expression of what repentance is, perhaps the greatest number of replies would be: "Repentance is sorrow for sin."

Though there can be no repentance without sorrow for sin, yet one can sorrow for sin a long time and never repent. You may shed many tears, and feel the lashings of conscience because of your wrongdoings, and not repent. It should be remembered that there are two kinds of sorrow.

SORROW OF THE WORLD.

JUDAS. "The sorrow of the world worketh death" (II Cor. 7:10). When Judas, who betrayed the Master (Mark 14:43), saw him in the hands of his enemies, condemned to death, his heart was filled with many regrets, the blood money burned his hands, and he cast it at the feet of the priests (Matt. 27:4, 5). Judas even confessed his sins, saying: "I have sinned in that I betrayed innocent blood" (Matt. 27:4). His sorrow must have been of the worldly sort; for instead of ending in a reformation of life, it resulted in his hanging himself. "The sorrow of the world worketh death" (II Cor. 7:10).

RICH RULER. A rich young ruler came to Christ (Matt. 19:16-22), inquiring what he must do to obtain eternal life. Having been told what to do, he went away sorrowful, for to comply with the conditions he must part with his wealth. There was no repentance in his heart—his sorrow was of the world. "The sorrow of the world worketh death."

THE DRUNKARD. The drunkard in his sober moments, realizing how he has dishonored himself and brought reproach on his parents and family, knowing the end of such a life, seeing that he is being shunned by his fellows and ostracized from the best society, is filled with sorrow; but he gets drunk again at the first opportunity. His sorrow was of the world. Sorrow is not repentance

GODLY SORROW IS NOT REPENTANCE

"Godly sorrow worketh repentance unto salvation" (II Cor. 7:10). When Peter was prosecuting the murderers of Christ, they cried out: "Brethren, what shall we do?" (Acts 2:37). There was sorrow in their hearts for the crime they had committed, but they had not repented, as is evidenced by the fact that Peter commanded them to repent (Acts 2:38). "Godly sorrow worketh repentance." The "godly sorrow" is not repentance, but it precedes and is necessary to repentance.

REFORMATION IS NOT REPENTANCE.

Paul preached "to them of Damascus first, and at Jerusalem, and throughout all the country of Judea, and also to the Gentiles, that they should repent and turn to God, doing works worthy of repentance" (Acts 26:20). They were commanded to "turn" to God, but turning to God came after their repentance. "Repent and turn from your idols" (Ezek. 14:6). Turning from idols, as well as turning from other wicked acts, is certainly a reformation, but this follows repentance.

TWO KINDS OF SORROW.

There is a vast difference between the "sorrow of the world" and "godly sorrow."

SORROW OF THE WORLD. The sorrow of the world worketh death. It is morbid and bitter, leaving one miserable with the goading of conscience, but gives no peace and promises no alleviation.

GODLY SORROW. Godly sorrow has God in it, for it rests on the assurance of divine clemency. Godly sorrow is sweet, cheering, inspiring with holy aspirations. It is wrought by the "goodness of God" (Rom. 2:5). Through God's word you learn how constantly Jehovah has extended his goodness to us to cause us to repent.

WHAT IS REPENTANCE?

It is not sorrow; it is not godly sorrow; it is not reformation.

It would be easy to give the meaning of the English world "repent," as it is defined by lexicographers, or to define the word "metanoeo," the corresponding Greek word; but perhaps it will be more satisfactory every way to have just the definition the Lord has given in his word.

THE TWO SONS.

"A man had two sons; and he came to the first, and said, Son, go work to-day in the vineyard. And he answered and said, I will not: but afterward he repented himself, and went. And he came to the second, and said likewise. And he answered and said, I go, sir: and went not" (Matt. 21:28-30).

The first son very positively declined to work in the vineyard, saying: "I will not." Just so long as such was his mental attitude, just so long as his *will* was opposed to the *will* of his father, he did not go. The father *willed* for the son to work in the vineyard; the son *willed* not to work in the vineyard. Later the son did go and work in the vineyard. Before he labored in the vineyard, what change had taken place in the son? Clearly he would not work in the vineyard so long as his *will* was opposed to the *will* of the father; so long as he *willed* not to labor in the vineyard he did not. But he did go and labor in the vineyard, which is evidence incontrovertible that he changed his will. Jesus says: "He repented himself, and went." (1) He did not go till he repented; (2) he did not go till he changed his will; (3) surely it is plain that repentance is a change of will, and results, always, in a changed life.

THE PRODIGAL SON.

"A certain man had two sons: and the younger of them said to his father, Father, give me the portion of thy substance that falleth to me. And he divided unto them his living. And not many days after, the younger son gathered all together and took his journey into a far country; and there he wasted his substance with riotous living. And when he had spent all, there arose a mighty famine in that country; and he began to be in want. And he went and joined himself to one of the citizens of that country; and he sent him into his fields to feed swine. And he would fain have filled his belly with the husks that the swine did eat: and no man gave unto him. But when he came to himself he said, How many hired servants of my father's have bread enough and to spare, and I perish here with hunger! I will arise and go to my father, and I will say unto him, Father, I have sinned against heaven, and in thy sight: I am no more worthy to be called thy son: make me as one of thy hired servants. And he arose, and came to his father. But while he was yet afar off, his father saw him, and was moved with compassion, and ran, and fell on his neck, and kissed him. And the son said unto him, Father, I have sinned against heaven, and in thy sight: I am no more worthy to be called thy son. But the father said to his servants, Bring forth quickly the best robe, and put it on him; and put a ring on his hand, and shoes on his feet: and bring the fatted calf, and kill it, and let us eat, and make merry: for this my son was dead, and is alive again; he was lost, and is found" (Luke 15:11-24).

Having reached his majority, the young man, dissatisfied with his limitations and surroundings and the orderings of his father's house, demanded his part of the estate. It was given him. Leaving home, he spent his money with a free hand. When his financial crisis came and the necessity for work arose, he found employment with a stock farmer. In a country far from home, with his bitter experience and menial position, he reflected on his folly. "He came to himself," and said: "I will arise, and go to my father." "And he arose, and came to his father." (1) The boy *willed* to leave his father's home. (2) He came to grief and sorrow. (3) He *willed* to return to his father's home. Clearly there was a change in his attitude; his *will* has undergone a change respecting his course of conduct. There is a new determination within him. (4) He immediately acts in keeping with the changed will. The life always conforms to the will.

Repentance is a change of will which always results in a reformation of life.

THE NINEVITES.

The Ninevites were a very wicked people (Jonah 1:2). Jonah was sent to warn them of the impending wrath of Jehovah (Jonah 3:2). They believed the preaching of Jonah (Jonah 3:5), humbled themselves in sackcloth and ashes (Jonah 3:5-8), and turned from their evil ways (Jonah 3:10). Christ says of them: "They repented at the preaching of Jonah" (Matt. 12:41). With them there was: (1) Belief of the preaching of Jonah. (2) Sorrow for the rebellious and sinful life. (3) Change of will respecting their conduct, which is repentance. (4) Reformation.

FEAR OF JUDGMENT.

Entering into that which causes repentance is an element of fear. "He commandeth men that they should all everywhere repent: inasmuch as he hath appointed a day in which he will judge the world" (Acts 17:30, 31). "Except ye repent, ye shall all in like manner perish" (Luke 13:3).

FRUITS OF REPENTANCE.

John the Baptist made reference to repentance as a tree, and called on those to whom he preached, to "bring forth fruits wothry of repentance" (Luke 3:8-11). They asked, "What must we do?" and John replied: "He that hath two coats, let him impart to him that hath none; and he that hath food, let him do likewise." To the publicans he said: "Extort no more than that which is appointed you." To the soldiers he said: "Exhort from no man by violence, neither accuse any one wrongfully; and be content with your wages."

RESTITUTION.

Restitution is a fruit of repentance.

A man stole a watch. Before the overt act of stealing there was the determination, the *will*, to steal the watch. In every case of repentance there is sorrow, godly sorrow, preceding the repentance. Is it possible for there to be sorrow for the theft of the watch if there is no disposition to return it? We have learned that repentance is a *change of will* as respects wrongdoing. The man *willed* to take and appropriate the watch, the property of another, thereby depriving the rightful owner of his goods. When he repents he *changes his will*. This being the case, he no longer *wills* to deprive the man of his property, and necessarily returns it. Restitution follows in every case of repentance when it is within the power to right the wrong of the past.

One cannot enter heaven with the stolen property of another in his possession.

Some years ago I preached a sermon in Vernon, Texas, on restitution. The next day a man came to me, reciting the following: "Five years ago I bought a five-dollar hat at a store in this town, having it charged. In the fall, when I wished to pay my account, I asked that the merchant give me an itemized statement of my account. In looking over the statement I found that the hat had not been charged, and I persuaded myself that it was no fault of mine that the hat was not charged to me and that I would say nothing to the merchant about it. I paid him the amount the statement called for, making no mention of the hat which he failed to charge."

What does the student think of this case?

Touching the matter of restitution, read Ex. 22:1-4; Lev. 6:5; Ezek. 35:15; Luke 19:1-19.

HOW LONG DOES IT TAKE ONE TO REPENT?

This question cannot be answered definitely, if the answer is desired in hours and minutes. It will take you just as long to repent as it will take you to *change your will* respecting a sinful life. Some men are quicker in thought and action than others. The Philippian jailer became a Christian within sixty minutes. This included his faith, repentance, and baptism. When Paul and Silas were committed to his charge he thrust them into the inner prison—he did not have enough of the milk of human kindness to lead him to wash their lacerated backs. Later came the earthquake, the sermon by Paul, then his faith, administering to the apostles in washing their backs. In this you see the fruits of repentance.

REPENTANCE IS DEMANDED OF ALL.

Repentance is demanded of each one who sins. Simon, though he was a member of the church, sinned, and he was commanded to repent (Acts 8:13-24).

THE ORDER OF REPENTANCE AND FAITH.

In the foregoing we have learned that he who will not repent cannot be saved.

The Methodists, Baptists, Presbyterians, and some others teach that one is saved the moment he believes—that simultaneous with faith is salvation. To hold this doctrine, and still contend that one must repent or he cannot be saved, they are put to the necessity of contending that repentance comes before faith.

There has been much needless controversy over the order of faith and repentance, for the order can no more be reversed than can be life and death.

Suppose one who teaches that repentance comes before faith goes as a missionary to China. His object is to make Christians out of the Chinese. To that end he preaches to them, telling them that they must have faith in Christ or they cannot be saved. Immediately he adds: "But you cannot believe in God and his Son, Christ, till you repent, and I now call on you to repent of your sins." The Chinaman replies: "What is repentance, and how does one repent, and of what must I repent?" The missionary answers: "You must repent of your sins, repent of having violated the law, you must determine to change your conduct respecting your violations of the law." With some heat the Chinaman replies: "I keep the law; I am a good citizen; I keep the laws of my ancestors and of my country." "O," says the missionary, "I do not mean that. I mean you must be sorry of the sins you have committed against the true and living God, and determine to serve him." In bewilderment the Chinaman replies: "Who is the God to whom you make reference, and why should I serve him?" The missionary replies: "He is the Creator of all things, the Ruler of the universe, and—" But how evident it must be to all that the missionary is trying to lead the Chinaman to believe in God, even before he can explain to him what repentance is, and what it demands. He is wrong in his theory, but his actions come in the natural order.

"Godly sorrow worketh repentance." "The goodness of God leadeth thee to repentance." How can his goodness lead me to repentance if I do not believe in him? Is it not a fact that I must believe in him before I can believe in his goodness to me?

Faith comes by hearing (Rom. 10:17). We preach

to people that they may hear and believe; but if one must repent before he can believe, there is no sense in preaching to those who have not repented. With those who teach that reepntance must come before faith, they should say: "Repent of your sins, and then we will preach the gospel to you."

If you were called on to preach to an infidel, what would your first work be? Would you call on him to repent first, or would you strive to get him to believe on God and his Christ?

In attempting to prove that repentance comes before faith, the following scriptures are brought into service: "The time is fulfilled, and the kingdom of God is at hand: repent ye, and believe in the gospel" (Mark 1:15). "John baptized with the baptism of repentance, saying unto the people that they should believe on him that should come after him, that is, on Jesus" (Acts 19:4). "Testifying both to Jews and to Greeks repentance toward God, and faith toward our Lord Jesus Christ" (Acts 20:21). The Jews, who were God's children under the first covenant, were taught to "repent and believe the gospel," to repent and believe on him that should come. When you remember that they were God's children, that they were in covenant relationship with him, but had broken the law, had sinned against Jehovah, and to this people, this people who believed in God, the message came: Ye have sinned against Jehovah, in whom you believe; and now, if you would be saved, repent of the sins you have committed against him, and by faith accept Christ, and you will be forgiven. Necessarily their repentance was to be directed toward Jehovah, against whom they had sinned. So Paul testified to the Jews and Greeks—people who believed in Jehovah and had sinned against him—that they must repent of the sins they had committed against him, and; now that Jesus has been crowned as King, they must have faith in him if they would be saved.

No one repents till he has sufficient faith to realize that he has sinned against Jehovah. The goodness of God leads to repentance (Rom. 2:4), but that is true only when one believes in God and his goodness.

DID PETER COMMAND THOSE WITHOUT FAITH TO BE BAPTIZED? If repentance comes before faith, then Peter commanded people who did not have faith to be baptized; for, when on the day of Pentecost the people cried, asking what to do, Peter replied: "Repent ye, and be baptized" (Acts 2:38). If these people were not believers at the time the command was delivered to them, it must follow that those without faith were commanded to be baptized. The truth, as all who read the Bible know, is: Peter had discoursed to these people, they had been led to believe what he preached, as is evidenced by the fact that they cried out, asking what to do. To these anxious inquirers to whom Peter had preached, these folk who believed, Peter said: "Repent ye."

* * *

TOPICS FOR INVESTIGATION AND DISCUSSION.

1. Restitution.
2. Repentance of the Ninevites.
3. Self-Justification Instead of Repentance.
4. "If I Have Sinned"—A Sham Repentance.
5. Self-Examination an Aid to Repentance.

* * *

QUESTIONS

1. Is sin universal?
2. What is sin?
3. Name some of the results of sin.
4. What the first sin man committed?
5. Does God save man in sin?
6. Who is the rightful ruler of man?

7. Can a law exist without a penalty?
8. Why is it right to punish the sinner?
9. Is there mercy in law?
10. Is God willing to save all?
11. Will all be saved?
12. Show that repentance was required in the Old Testament.
13. Why was John called "The Baptist?"
14. In what country did he preach?
15. What did he preach?
16. Who were the parents of John the Baptist?
17. Why was he beheaded?
18. Give some quotations from the language of Jesus requiring repentance.
19. Show that the Great Commission requires repentance.
20. Why important to know what repetnance is?
21. Is sorrow repentance?
22. How many kinds of sorrow?
23. Can one repent without sorrow in the heart?
24. What is sorrow of the world?
25. What does sorrow of the world do for one?
26. Did Judas repent?
27. Narrate the history of the rich ruler.
28. Has the man who repeatedly gets drunk repented?
29. May he not be filled with sorrow and not repent?
30. What kind of sorrow works repentance?
31. What the difference between repentance and reformation?
32. Give a quotation showing that repentance comes before turning from sin.
33. What the difference between godly sorrow and sorrow of the world?
34. What does godly sorrow have in it?
35. What is repentance?
36. Give narrative of the two sons.
37. What the evidence that the men repented?
38. Tell the story of the prodigal son.
39. What the evidence that he repented?
40. Give history of Ninevah, when established, the size, location.
41. What the condition of Ninevah now?
42. Give history of Jonah.
43. What did Christ say about the Ninevites?
44. In what is the evidence that they repented?

REPENTANCE

45. What relationship does the fear of judgment bear to repentance?
46. Name some fruits of repentance.
47. What is restitution?
48. Does God demand restitution?
49. If one does not restore, has he repented?
50. What of the man who did not pay for the hat?
51. Had he died without paying for the hat, what?
52. How long does it take to repent?
53. Who must repent?
54. Show that reepntance cannot come before faith in the conversion of heathens. Illustrate by missionary in China.
55. In attempting to convert an infidel, what would you do first? Why?
56. Explain why repentance is sometimes mentioned before faith.

PARTAKERS OF THE DIVINE NATURE.

LESSON TEXT: "Yea, and for this very cause adding on your part all diligence, in your faith supply virtue; and in your virtue knowledge; and in your knowledge self-control; and in your self-control patience; and in your patience godliness; and in your godliness brotherly kindness; and in your brotherly kindness love" (II Peter 1:5-7).

LEADING UP TO THE LESSON.

"YEA, AND FOR THIS VERY CAUSE." For what cause? If we miss this point, we lose the real lesson. Add certain things. Why? There is a reason, a cause, for this admonition, and to learn its significance and to get the benefit of this lesson in "addition," we must begin back a little to see what is to be accomplished by adding these things. To this end, let us note carefully the thoughts presented in the preceding verses.

"A LIKE PRECIOUS FAITH." An equally precious faith (see marginal reading in the American Standard Version). Although Peter had seen the Lord and was able to speak and write by inspiration, the faith of these brethren who had not so much as seen the Lord was just as precious as his. *"The knowledge of God and of Jesus our Lord."* The knowledge of God does not mean what God knows, but that which we know, or has been revealed, about him. In verse 8 Peter says: "For if these things are yours and abound, they make you to be not idle nor unfruitful unto the knowledge of our Lord Jesus Christ." We may be barren or unfruitful in our knowledge of God, but we can neither be fruitful nor unfruitful in what God knows. Peter says: "But grow in the grace and knowledge of our Lord and Savior Jesus Christ" (II Peter 3:18). We may grow in our knowledge of Christ, but we cannot grow in what he knows. Hence in verse 2 we learn that God's grace and peace will be multiplied to us along as we learn more of him.

"ALL THINGS THAT PERTAIN TO LIFE AND GODLINESS." Not only has God given us all things necessary to life and godliness, but also all things that pertain to life and godliness. And this has been given to us "through the knowledge of him that called us"—that is, all things that pertain to life and godliness have been given to us through the knowledge revealed to us in the Bible. Anything in our religion which cannot be found in this knowledge which God has revealed to us does not pertain to life and godliness. *"Whereby"*—that is, in these "all things that pertain unto life and godliness"—*"he hath granted unto us his precious and exceeding great promises."* These promises are many, but may be summed up in these two—namely, salvation from sin and becoming children of God. *"That through these ye may become partakers of the divine nature."* We become partakers of the divine nature only as to goodness and holiness—the perfection of character. We are made partakers of the divine nature through the promises of God. But how do God's promises make us better? The mere fact that God has made promises to us has never made any one any better, for some are as wicked as they would have been had God never made a promise to anyone. How, then, do they make us better? There is nothing in an unconditional promise to make any one better. But God intends for his religion to make us better here, and for that reason he suspends his promises upon conditions the performance of which makes us better. He, in effect, says to us: "If you would enjoy these precious promises, quit your sins and let me guide your life." This stimulates us to better living. This harmonizes with Paul: "Come ye out from among them, and be ye separate, saith the Lord. And touch no unclean thing; and I will receive you, and will be to you a Father, and ye shall be to me sons and daughters, saith the Lord Almighty" (II Cor. 6:17, 18). The command: "Separate yourself from unclean things." The promises: "I will receive you; will be a Father to you; you shall be children of God." Paul immediately adds: "Having therefore these promises, beloved, let us cleanse ourselves from all defilement of flesh and spirit, perfecting holiness in the fear of God" (I Cor. 7:1).

THE CAUSE.

"Yea, and for this very cause"—that is, to accomplish this very end, namely, to become partakers of the divine nature—"adding on your part," etc. The divine nature possesses certain characteristics. These must be added, that we may become partakers of this divine nature. It is a mistake to represent these elements as so many steps in a stairway or ladder upon which we may climb into the eternal kingdom. In climbing a ladder we have each rung behind us as we step on to the next, and have no further use for them unless we aim to come down again. Is that true with reference to these Christian graces? Do we leave faith behind when we mount the rung of courage, and so on to the last, from which we are supposed to step into heaven? That is absurd. The fact is, these graces are cumulative—each is to be added till we reach the sum total of all.

These verses give us, rather, God's formula for the divine nature. It is as if the apostle had said: "If you would be a partaker of the divine nature, you must diligently add to your faith certain graces, you must compound your character by this formula." If the formula is diligently followed, the result is certain and definite. Being a faithful Christian is not an accident. When the chemist diligently compounds elements after a given formula, the result is no accident, but definite and certain. God says to us: "If you would be a partaker of the divine nature, here is the formula; compound the elements diligently." Faith is the base; other elements must be added. But diligence is required; otherwise the result will be disappointing.

DILIGENCE is necessary to success in any worthy undertaking. There is too much careless indifference, too much slothfulness, too much of the hit-or-miss style of Christian living. While diligence is recognized as necessary in business, how few recognize that it is just as necessary in Christian living!

VIRTUE. "IN YOUR FAITH SUPPLY VIRTUE." Virtue is generally here understood to mean manliness, or courage, the disposition to stand for what we espouse. What is your faith worth if you have not courage to stand up for it or live it? But courage is not blustering and blowing about what we believe and what we will do. It does not mean that we shut our eyes to danger—that is foolhardiness. It does not even mean the absence of fear. Perhaps no man was ever more courageous than Paul, yet to the Corinthians he said: "I was with you in weakness, and in fear, and in much trembling" (I Cor 2:3). This story illustrates the point: It is said that during a battle an officer who was commanding a division of the army was sitting on his horse, pale and fearful, directing his men, while the bullets flew thick and fast. Another officer, dashing up, said: "You look scared." "I am scared," said he; "and if you were scared half as bad as I am, you would run." That is courage—when a man realizes his danger, and yet stands at the post of duty. Any weakling can stand his ground when he is not scared, but it takes a brave man to stay with his duty when he is scared.

KNOWLEDGE. "IN YOUR VIRTUE KNOWLEDGE." Of course a person must have some knowledge, just as he must have some courage, to ever become a Christian, but he needs to advance in both. Courage without knowledge may become very hurtful. Without knowledge courage may lead a person to do things hurtful both to himself and the church. And yet few Christians seem to realize that God commands them to add knowledge, yet it is one of the fundamental requirements, one of the essential elements of the divine nature. No one ignorant of the will of God can hope to live the Christian life.

"My people are destroyed for lack of knowledge: because thou hast rejected knowledge, I will also reject thee" (Hos. 4:6). Jesus said: "Take my yoke upon you, and learn of me" (Matt. 11:29). "For when by reason of the time ye ought to be teachers, ye have need again that some one teach you the rudiments of the first principles of the oracles of God" (Heb. 5:12). This shows that God expects all his children to so study his will that in a reasonable length of time they will be able to teach others.

TEMPERANCE. "IN YOUR KNOWLEDGE TEMPERANCE." Temperance is self-control, especially with reference to our lusts. The fight against strong drink adopted the word "temperance" and narrowed its meaning to abstinence from intoxicating liquors, but its meaning was not so restricted in the New Testament. Temperance means self-control. A person does not control himself when he indulges in any excess or in anything that is hurtful to him. Temperance, then, signifies moderate indulgence in those things that are good for the body and total abstinence from hurtful things.

PATIENCE. "IN YOUR TEMPERANCE PATIENCE." "Patience" is a much-abused word. Too often patience is thought to be a non-resisting, quiet spirit that, without complaint or protest, submits to any sort of conditions or circumstances. But patience is not complacency or serenity. A person may be undisturbed when things go wrong simply because he does not care. Let us not mistake indifference for patience. "Ye have heard of the patience of Job," says James. And so you have. Have you ever considered the quality of his patience? Did you ever read the book of Job? Did he strike you as an example of patience? He had lost all his flocks and herds, his servants and children, and had become sorely afflicted with boils. Crushed in spirit, heartsore and full of grief, he sat down among the ashes. His would-be friends heard of his grief and came to him. Seven days they sat in silence, with not a word of comfort or reproof. Job's long-pent-up feelings burst forth in a tirade of cursing against his day. His friends then argued with him, and told him that his meanness had got him into all this trouble. He blurted out in irony: "No doubt but ye are the people, and wisdom shall die with you" (Job 12:2). That does not indicate what some people call patience. And his good wife, who had looked on him in his afflictions and sufferings till she could stand it no longer, said to him: "Dost thou still hold fast thine intergrity? renounce God, and die." She seemed to think that if he would renounce God, God would kill him, and that this would be the quickest way to end his afflictions. But Job replied: "Thou speakest as one of the foolish women speak." That would appear to some as an outburst of impatience; but it is because we mistake the meaning of the word "patience," and we forget that despite all of Job's fuming and fussing he is recorded by inspiration as an example of patience. His patience is seen in that, though he had lost his property and was bereaved of his children and had become afflicted all over with boils, and though his friends had now become his accusers and his wife had seemed to reach the end of her endurance and had called upon him to renounce God, he could look up through the darkness and despair surrounding him and say: "Though he slay me, yet will I trust him." "I will hold on to God if I lose all my property; I will hold on to him if I lose all my children and if my friends forsake me and if my wife gives up in despair; and I will still trust him, though he slay me." That is patience.

"Patience" comes from a word that means "to remain under," and carries with it the idea of remaining steadfast under any kind of hardships or difficulties. Patience, or steadfastness, is a quality much needed in present-day Christians. We are too ready to quit under any provocation or difficulty. It is easy to serve God when everything goes on like a sweet song, but the Christian that is worth while is the one who holds on under all kinds of adverse conditions or circumstances.

GODLINESS. " IN YOUR PATIENCE GODLINESS." "Godliness" does not mean Godlikeness. The Greek word translated *godliness* is thus defined by Thayer: *"Reverence, respect; in the Bible everywhere piety toward God, godliness."* Godliness is piety, reverence. It grows out of a feeling of dependence upon God and a deep regard for his majesty and glory. It is also manifested in a proper respect and deference for that which belongs to God or pertains to him. We are lacking in reverence. Majesty and power is not ascribed to God, his name is spoken lightly, his word is used in jokes and jests, the blood-bought church is not thought of as the body of Christ, and the name of God and Christ is blasphemed. Even preachers sometimes profane the name of God in the pulpit. This is done when a preacher lightly and flippantly says: "Before God, brethren."

But reverence, like other virtues, must be learned. It should begin in the home. Parents should teach their children to respect them, to properly reverence father and mother. If reverence is not learned in the home, it is not likely to develop later. The habit of reverence, the principle of reverence, must be instilled in the child. If not, he will grow up devoid of respect for parents, for his teachers in school, and for the laws of the land. Such a one is most likely to be without reverence for God—a hardened, ungodly sinner. Ungodliness is irreverence, impiety. A godly man, a pious man, may fall into wrong, but his reverence for God will most likely restore him. But there is little hope for the redemption of an ungodly sinner.

"BROTHERLY KINDNESS." Thayer defines the Greek: "*The love of brothers (or sisters), brotherly love; in the New Testament, the love which Christians cherish for each other as brethren.*" Genuine love manifests itself in different ways. The mother through the long hours of the night will tenderly watch over the sick child, or will tenderly bind up his bruised toes or wounded fingers, and sympathize with him in his griefs and disappointments; but genuine mother love will also be stern and unbending when the occasion demands and will inflict punishment when the need arises, all the while doing what under the circumstances seems best. True love looks not to the present pleasure, but to the ultimate good of the person loved. Hence, to love the brethren does not mean that you must flatter them, or even to always speak words to please them. We must do them good—help them in their needs, comfort them in their sorrows, and tenderly nourish the downcast and broken-hearted; and if they fall into wrong, we must seek to reclaim them, and, if necessary, rebuke them sharply. Jesus rebuked Peter sharply (Matt. 16:22, 23), and Paul, charged Timothy: "Them that sin reprove in the sight of all, that the rest also may be in fear" (I Tim. 5:20). The Lord loves his children, yet he says: "My son, regard not lightly the chastening of the Lord, nor faint when thou art reproved of him; for whom the Lord loveth he chasteneth, and scourgeth every son whom he receiveth" (Heb. 12:5, 6).

LOVE. To love of the brethren we must add universal love—love for all men. And this love, too, must be active. God so loved the world that he *gave* his only begotten Son. We must so love man that we will give the best that is in us to serve man's best interests. Love transforms duty into opportunity, and makes sacrifice satisfying and pleasurable service. It takes the drudgery from daily toil, and gives a feeling of gladness that we are able to share in the uplift and betterment of mankind.

SUMMARY. Faith is the base to which all these elements are added. It is the beginning of the life divine. But too many are satisfied with being nominal, or professed, Christians. A small degree of faith, kept as a secret in your own heart, requires no courage to so exist, and finally perishes for lack of cultivation. For faith to assert itself requires courage. But courage needs the guidance of knowledge; otherwise it is mere foolhardiness. But knowledge is worthless if we give sway to all our appetites and passions. Hence, we must add temperance, or self-control. But this effort to add self-control, this battle against passions, lust, and selfishness, is a fierce conflict, and requires sustained effort. Hence, the need of patience, or steadfastness. But we must not allow our victories over self nor our steadfastness of character to develop a feeling of self-sufficiency. We must take God into account, and realize our dependence on him; for it is in him that we live, move, and have our being. We must add reverence, or godliness. But it is not enough that we cultivate self

PARTAKERS OF THE DIVINE NATURE

and reverence God. In the busy field of service our brothers in the Lord are crying for help; we must not forget them. Duty calls, and brotherly love leads us to share their struggles, trials, and sufferings. In our love for our brethren let us not become clannish and forget the great mass of unconverted sinners. It is possible for us to become selfish in our love for the church and to develop a sort of family pride. Such a one does not think of leading men to Christ for their own sakes and because they need salvation, but he thinks of the world as a quarry out of which he may extract material to help build up the church and make it greater and more glorious. But the Christian must outgrow that trait; he must cultivate love for men and seek to reclaim them from sin and ruin because he loves them. Hence, to brotherly love add universal love.

THE RESULTS. The immediate result of compounding these elements into your character is that you become a partaker of the divine nature, but the ultimate result is that there shall be given to you an abundant entrance into the everlasting kingdom of God.

* * *

TOPICS FOR INVESTIGATION AND DISCUSSION.

The Preciousness of Faith.
What God's Promises Mean to Me.
The Need of Bible Study.
The Uses and Abuses of the Bible.
This Life a Preparation for the Next.

* * *

QUESTIONS.

1. To whom did Peter write?
2. What is faith?
3. What difference between faith and belief?
4. What is meant by "precious faith?"
5. What is meant by "the knowledge of God?"

6. What is the meaning of "all things that pertain to life and godliness?"
7. How and where are these things given us?
8. In the light of this passage, what do you think of human creeds?
9. Can you mention some practices of religious neighbors not authorized by the Bible?
10. Name some of the "precious and exceeding great promises."
11. How do we become partakers of the divine nature?
12. How does a promise make one better?
13. Are these promises conditional?
14. Can you name some unconditional promises of the Bible?
15. How do we "cleanse ourselves?"
16. Name elements necessary to partaking of divine nature.
17. Is the illustration of climbing a ladder good?
18. What is diligence?
19. Give some illustrations of diligence in business.
20. Give an example of your diligence in religion.
21. What is the meaning of virtue?
22. Give an instance in your life where courage was lacking.
23. Can a courageous man be afraid?
24. What the necessity of knowledge in religious matters?
25. How is knowledge acquired?
26. How are people destroyed for lack of knowledge?
27. Show mistakes, sins through lack of knowledge.
28. Can one sin through ignorance?
29. Does law, human or divine, excuse man for his ignorance?
30. What is temperance?
31. Is indulgence in a practice necessary to temperance?
32. Name some ways in which one may fail to be temperate.
33. Does temperance demand "total abstinence?" What?
34. What is patience?
35. Does waiting for Brother X to come show patience?
36. Who was Job?
37. Tell of Job's afflictions.
38. How long did Job and his friends sit in mourning?
39. What the names of Job's three friends?
40. What advice did the three friends give him?
41. What did Job's wife say?

PARTAKERS OF THE DIVINE NATURE

42. How did Job regard his birthday?
43. What is godliness?
44. What about using God's name as a jest or as a byword?
45. What is meant by brotherly kindness?
46. How is brotherly kindness manifested?
47. What is love?
48. What is it to love your enemies?

www.ingramcontent.com/pod-product-compliance
Lightning Source LLC
LaVergne TN
LVHW011913080426
835508LV00007BA/506